# FOR THE LOVE OF
# RUGBY

FOR THE LOVE OF RUGBY

First published as *The Joy of Rugby* in 2014

This revised and expanded edition copyright © Summersdale Publishers Ltd, 2017

Images © Shutterstock

All rights reserved.

Steven Gauge has asserted his right to be identified as the author of this work in accordance with sections 77 and 78 of the Copyright, Designs and Patents Act 1988.

Summersdale Publishers Ltd
46 West Street
Chichester
West Sussex
PO19 1RP
UK

www.summersdale.com

Printed and bound in the Czech Republic

ISBN: 978-1-84953-999-9

Substantial discounts on bulk quantities of Summersdale books are available to corporations, professional associations and other organisations. For details contact general enquiries: telephone: +44 (0) 1243 771107, fax: +44 (0) 1243 786300 or email: enquiries@summersdale.com.

# FOR THE LOVE OF
## RUGBY
### A COMPANION

**STEVEN GAUGE**

summersdale

# CONTENTS

••••••••••••••••••••••••••••••••••••••••••

# INTRODUCTION

When Mrs Webb Ellis lost her husband at the Battle of Albuera in 1811, during the Peninsular War, she decided to move to Rugby in Warwickshire. This allowed her two sons, William and Thomas, to take advantage of a free education at Rugby School, offered to boys living within 10 miles of the school clock tower. Her decision, combined with William's apparent inclination to 'take unfair advantage at football', has given the world a wonderful game that is now played in over 100 countries around the world.

According to a letter written in 1880 from Matthew Bloxam to *The Meteor*, the Rugby School magazine, William Webb Ellis caught the ball during a game of football in the latter half of 1823 and, instead of retiring back down the pitch and kicking the ball as the rules then required, he 'rushed forwards with the ball in his hands towards the opposite goal'. Today there is a bronze statue beside the school and a plaque on a wall commemorating the young man and describing how he 'with a fine disregard for the rules of football as played in his time first took the ball in his arms and ran with it thus originating the distinctive feature of the rugby game'.

There is something about the phrase 'with a fine disregard for the rules' that sums up everything we love about rugby.

One can easily imagine a predictable kick-around on a wet Wednesday afternoon in Warwickshire being brought to life by a spirited young chap deciding that the game would be a whole lot more interesting if the players could make use of all four limbs. The thought that, rather than punishing or suppressing this burst of youthful exuberance, Webb Ellis's peers decided to play along with him, creating a new game, is delightfully uplifting and life-affirming. Even more cheering when viewed from an age of bureaucracy and regulation, early games of rugby were entirely referee-free zones. Rather than waiting for a man with a whistle to intervene, play generally continued, with any disagreements being settled by a gentlemanly understanding between the captains.

It's not only the rules that get treated with a fine disregard, of course. Rugby breeds a certain sort of player who will throw his or her whole body into the game with fine disregard for personal safety, decorum or dignity. Once a week, rugby allows people to test themselves physically by launching into huge tackles, diving into great heaving, rolling mauls and unleashing powerful runs through determined defences – all in the interests of carrying an odd-shaped ball over a white line painted on the grass. I don't know if that's quite what Webb Ellis originally had in mind, but he and his school friends started something wonderful and we love them for it.

Indeed, there is also something very lovable about a game that brings together towns, cities, regions and nations to cheer on the finest players of the game and share with them every impact, every kick and every scrum. Whether watching a local club in a lowly league from the touchline, or an international fixture in one of the world's great stadiums, the collective experience, the shared humour and the sheer pleasure of watching the sport is much the same.

You can turn up to many a rugby club on a Sunday morning and see hundreds of children from age five to 18 discovering the joy of rugby. They might start off with the contact-free, tag-and-touch version of the game, saving nervous parents from premature grey hairs and intermittent heart failure. After a few years, however, they are desperate to try tackling, scrummaging, rucking and mauling as they grow in confidence, stature and strength. On a cold, muddy weekend you cannot force anyone to play rugby; they would only do it if they loved the game.

Some of us come to rugby later in life. I only really discovered the game at the age of 35, when I found a sport that was, to my surprise and delight, more than welcoming to someone of my age and with my lack of discernible talent. In clubs all over the country, third-, fourth- and fifth-team captains will warmly embrace anyone new who wants to try out the game. Rugby finds something to love about everyone whatever shape or size they might be. With larger bodies finding a home in the forwards and thinner, faster types free to run around in the backs, rugby has the ability to find a place on the pitch for almost anyone.

Even after the final whistle has blown, our love affair with rugby continues. The feeling as you walk off the pitch after a game, and shake hands warmly with the same people whom only a few minutes earlier you were trying to tear down to the ground, is a mixture of relief, exhaustion and contentment.

There is a sense that you have been through a very raw and wholehearted primal experience, and that you have very much earned the beer that awaits you in the clubhouse bar.

Rugby, it turns out, is more than just a game; it is a celebration of what we can achieve physically as individuals, together as a team and a club, and sometimes, as those World Cup competitions come around every four years, as a nation. So whether you play the game, watch the game or are just trying to fathom why so many other people do, take some time to sit back and enjoy these chapters celebrating our mighty sport.

# TIMELINE

• • • • • • • • • • • • • • • • • • • • • • • • • • • • • • • • • • • • • • • •

Rugby is more than just a game of two halves. It is now a game of nearly two centuries. Its history has shaped not just the ball, but every aspect of the modern game. Here for your easy reference and reflection are the key moments that have helped to create the game that we love today.

**1823**  William Webb Ellis first picks up the ball and runs with it

**1839**  Rugby School House team adopts a uniform of red velvet caps for a game being watched by Princess Adelaide

**1843**  Guy's Hospital Rugby Club formed

**1845**  First set of rules published by Rugby School

**1871**  Rugby Football Union (RFU) formed

**1875**  Teams reduced to 15 a side

**1878**  Cardiff side invent the 'flying half back', which later becomes the fly half

**1883**  First sevens tournament in Melrose, Scotland

**1884**  First New Zealand tour to New South Wales, Australia

**1885**     Referee's whistle introduced

**1886**     International Rugby Board formed (England refuse to join until 1890)

**1888**     British and Irish Lions tour Australia and New Zealand

**1893**     Payments to players to compensate for loss of earnings blocked by the RFU

**1895**     22 Northern clubs break away to allow player payments, leading to the development of the alternative code of Rugby League

**1903**     New Zealand play their first international game against Australia

**1905**     All Blacks tour British Isles

**1907**     RFU committee member Billy Williams buys 10 ¼ acres of market garden in Twickenham, south-west London

**1910**     First international played at Twickenham (England v Wales)

**1938**     First international broadcast live on TV (England v Scotland)

**1939–45**     During the Second World War Twickenham was used as a civil defence depot and the car park was dug up for allotments

**1968**     Replacement of injured players allowed – two per team

**1969**     Anti-apartheid demonstrations as South Africa tour UK

# TIMELINE

**1987**     First World Cup Tournament held in Australia and New Zealand

**1992**     The modern points system was introduced (try = 5 points; penalty = 3; drop goal = 3; conversion = 2)

**1995**     Rugby Union becomes professional

**2003**     England become the first Northern Hemisphere side to win the World Cup

**2006**     Twickenham South Stand reopens, taking the ground's capacity to 82,000

**2015**     Eighth Rugby World Cup Tournament staged in England and is won by New Zealand

**2016**     Rugby returns to the Olympics in Rio, with Australia winning the women's sevens and Fiji winning the men's sevens

*In 1823, William Webb Ellis first picked up the ball in his arms and ran with it. And for the next 156 years forwards have been trying to work out why.*

**SIR TASKER WATKINS, PRESIDENT OF THE WELSH RUGBY UNION**

# RUGBY IN NUMBERS

### 7.73 MILLION
men, women and children playing the game
in World Rugby Member Unions

### 120
countries where rugby is played

### 2.47 MILLION
tickets sold across 48 matches in the 2015 Rugby World Cup

### 6,000
volunteers who supported the 2015 Rugby World Cup

### 95 PER CENT
percentage of available seats filled across all
the games in the 2015 Rugby World Cup

## 120 MILLION

worldwide viewing audience of the 2015 Rugby World Cup final

·····

## 22 ST 9 LBS

weight of the heaviest player, Uini (pronounced Weeny)
Atonio of New Zealand, in the 2015 Rugby World Cup

·····

## 7,098

the average number of metres covered by
a scrum half in the course of a game

·····

## 3

most red cards handed out in an international, in a game
between South Africa and Canada in the 1995 World Cup

·····

## 1,179

points scored by Jonny Wilkinson in an England shirt in
an international career lasting from 1998 to 2011

·····

## 152

biggest international victory margin, jointly held by Argentina,
who defeated Paraguay by 152–0 in 2002, and Japan, who
beat Chinese Taipei by 155–3 that same year

·····

## 40 YEARS AND 243 DAYS

age of the oldest player to turn out for his international side,
Kevin Wirachowsky, when he came on as a substitute for
Canada against New Zealand Maoris in 2003

# A GLOBAL PHENOMENON

> **❝** *I love rugby because it's a sociocultural experience; travelling the world and meeting people ... actually it's more for the frequent flyer points.* **❞**
>
> **JAMES HOLBECK, AUSTRALIAN RUGBY PLAYER AND COACH**

More so than many other sports, rugby is at its heart an international beast, a citizen of the world. Whilst the club game is important, with local community clubs attracting great loyalty and larger professional sides attracting large crowds, the primary focus for players and spectators alike are the international Test matches. The game may have started its life on the playing fields of the English public schools, but many of us love rugby because of the passionate national rivalries and the international fixtures that shape every season. The game reaches its widest audience around the times of international Test matches and tours rather than through club fixtures and national leagues. At every level of the game rugby feels like an international sport, with friendships and rivalries stretching all around the globe.

Playing teams from other countries and cultures is as much a part of the experience and joy of the game as the smell of Deep

Heat in the changing room before a game or the drinking and singing afterwards. For many sides, from schoolboy teams to local community clubs, the international tours and exchanges often take on a far greater significance than any domestic competition.

The game has spread from its birthplace in England to all continents (games have even been played between the research scientists of different nationalities at Scott Base in Antarctica), and every nation that picks up the oval ball adds a new dimension and spirit to the game. We will look at the international characteristics of some of the different nations that play the game, but we must start where the game itself began, in England.

# ENGLAND

*Forasmuch as there is great noise in the city caused by hustling over large balls, from which many evils may arise, which God forbid, we command and forbid on behalf of the king, on pain of imprisonment, such game to be used in the city in future.*

**PROCLAMATION FROM EDWARD II, 1314**

Long before the day when William Webb Ellis picked up the ball at an elite public school, there were plenty of common folk enjoying the simple pleasure of throwing a ball around in a competitive fashion. In medieval Britain, villages staged games where huge mobs would compete to carry an inflated pig's bladder from one side of the town to another.

The purest form of the game survives today in places like Ashbourne in Derbyshire, where, every Shrove Tuesday, 'Uppers' (those born north of the River Henmore) compete against 'Downers' (those born on the southern side) to get a ball from the car park in the centre of the town to one of two mills on the outskirts. There are few rules and the game can last for up to eight hours, but if no one has scored a goal by 10 p.m. the ball must be returned to the Green Man and Black's Head public house for safekeeping until the following year.

Village folk continued kicking and throwing balls around for a few more centuries, and the games appear to have found their way into the English public schools and from there into the universities. The games were still pretty rough and in 1303 an Oxford student called Thomas of Salisbury found his brother Adam dead, apparently as a result of a football game in the High Street against some Irish students.

Ball games got themselves banned every so often but over the next few centuries public school headmasters began to see the virtues and benefits of getting their young charges to burn off some excess energy by chasing around after a ball full of wind. A little light regulation was introduced along with referees, positions and coaches, and different schools developed their own versions of the sport.

In 1845 three boys at Rugby School got together and produced the first printed set of rules. Other schools began to play the game according to the Rugby School rules. Cheltenham College were invited up to Rugby for the first inter-school match, which they duly won. Then rugby clubs began to be formed as the boys from the school moved away and entered employment.

While Webb Ellis became a vicar, some of his contemporaries joined the medical profession; the first rugby club to get itself organised enough to have an inaugural annual general meeting was at Guy's Hospital in London. No doubt the injuries thus sustained gave them some useful subjects to practise upon as they honed their surgical skills.

## THE ASSOCIATION GAME

In 1863, a Football Association was formed by clubs that wanted to rule out the practice of hacking, or kicking an opponent in the leg. The game those clubs played according to 'association rules' gradually evolved into the game that involves kicking a spherical ball, marrying Spice Girls and regularly delivering theatrical performances for the referee while complaining that your opponent has kicked you in the shin. This game was hereafter known by most people as football, by Americans as soccer and by rugby pedants as 'the association game'.

Rugby clubs sprang up all around the country. Barnes Rugby Football Club apparently formed in 1839, but they didn't get round to writing a match report until 1862. The old boys of Blackheath School had been playing rugby on the heath from 1858 and in 1862 decided to knock up a club constitution and open up the membership to the wider public. In 1857 former Rugby School pupil William Mather put together a side made up of his old schoolmates and invited another old schoolfriend and school captain to bring over a similar side from Manchester. An exhibition game was played in front of a large crowd at Liverpool Cricket Ground, and the groundsman marked out the pitch using white chalk. Clubs were formed in Liverpool and Manchester as a result.

All this activity started to need organising, and the well-thumbed copies of the original Rugby School rules were presumably beginning to look a little dog-eared. The Rugby Football Union was convened and had its very first meeting at the Pall Mall Restaurant behind Trafalgar Square in London on 26 January 1871. The restaurant is no longer there, but there is a plaque at the site to mark its significance to the game. Three lawyers, who also happened to be old boys from Rugby School, were given the task of redrafting the regulations. As they were lawyers, their version became laws rather than rules, as rugby pedants will remind you at every available opportunity.

Now, the eagle-eyed rugby lovers among you will have noticed the emergence of the word 'union'. The attempt to unite the sport into one family with one set of rules (sorry, laws) was embodied by the creation, in the shadow of Nelson's Column, of the Rugby Football Union. However, it wasn't long before the union began to fracture and an alternative version of the game emerged.

> *I'm 49, I've had a brain haemorrhage and a triple bypass and I could still go out and play a reasonable game of rugby union. But I wouldn't last 30 seconds in rugby league.*
> **GRAHAM LOWE, NEW ZEALAND RUGBY LEAGUE COACH**

Charles Darwin published his book *On the Origin of Species* in 1859, including his theories of natural selection. It had taken a sober and academic tour of the Galápagos Islands and the surrounding area to gather the evidence to support his theories of adaptation and survival. However, he could have stayed at home, had a beer or two and observed the evolution of two very distinct subspecies of *Homo rugbyus*. The sport of rugby in the north of England was having to adapt to a different economic environment, and was about to branch off and give birth to an entirely new variety of the game – rugby league.

## PAY UP OR ELSE...

Towards the end of the nineteenth century rugby was becoming hugely popular in northern cities, with vast crowds paying to watch teams compete. The clubs were generating substantial revenues, but none of it was allowed to find its way into the players' wallets as the game's regulators strictly enforced a code of amateurism.

The players, mostly drawn from traditional working-class trades, would also struggle to earn a living if they were injured in the course of a game. A proposal was put to the Rugby Football Union to allow clubs to pay players for 'broken time', to compensate them for any time missed from work.

The RFU had been formed by public schoolboys, many of whom didn't have to worry about maintaining a steady income. Dominated by southern clubs with aristocratic and aspirational middle-class members, it voted down the proposal and northern clubs were suspended if they were suspected of paying players.

In August 1895, 22 clubs met in the George Hotel in Huddersfield and, after three hours of private deliberation, resolved to form a breakaway Northern Rugby Football Union, specifically to permit the payment of players for broken time. The game played from then on in the northern leagues became known as rugby league, and the game played under the auspices of the original RFU became known as rugby union.

## A DIFFERENT LEAGUE

The two branches of the game evolved and developed in their own different ways. In rugby league, the game became much more open as the scrum stopped being a monumental battle to see which pack could push the other off the ball. Instead, it has become a device for tying up a few players in the centre of the pitch to give the others in the team a little more room to run around. Each tackle in rugby league is ended when the attacking player is deemed by the referee to have been held.

With paying crowds to entertain and salaries to pay, rugby league needed to be open and entertaining, with everyone able to see what was happening within the game. Rugby union, on the other hand, remaining a strictly amateur sport, retained rucks, mauls and scrums where the so-called dark arts of forward play are largely hidden from the spectators' view.

Rugby union remained an amateur pursuit for the next hundred years. During that time, no rugby league player was ever allowed to play rugby union, while rugby union players were banned from ever playing rugby union again if they were tempted to switch codes and play the northern game.

# SCOTLAND

When they were not squeezing the air out of inflated animal bladders and through some very noisy pipes, the Scots were fond of kicking or throwing inflated animal bladders around in various forms of early football. It didn't take long for the Rugby School set of rules for doing that in a slightly more structured way to make it north of the border. The Edinburgh Academy adopted the game in 1851 and other schools soon followed. Dr Hely Hutchinson Almond, the headmaster at Loretto School in Musselburgh, is credited with creating the passing aspect of the game. At that time the sport was played with 20 players per side and most of them spent most of their time in a giant seething, steaming scrum. If the ball did emerge players would grab it and run as fast and as far as they could before being 'collared' and then 'hacked' off the ball. H. H. Almond encouraged his boys to pass the ball to one another to confuse the opposition, much to the disapproval of the other Edinburgh headmasters.

H. H. Almond also has the distinction of being the official to preside over the first ever rugby international fixture, which was between Scotland and England in Edinburgh in 1871. The catalyst for the fixture was a somewhat irascible Scottish reaction to having been defeated in a football international against England a year earlier. The Scots claimed that rugby football was the preferred game north of the border and so challenged the English to put together a side. Twenty English players were assembled, including John Clayton from the Liverpool club, whose training regime consisted of a 4-mile run every day for a month with his large Newfoundland dog acting as pacemaker and personal trainer.

With 13 forwards on each side, the game largely turned into an extended maul with the backs rarely getting a look-in. In those days points were awarded solely for kicking the ball through the goalposts, either from a drop kick or from a converted try. There were no points for touching the ball down over the line, an achievement which simply qualified the side for a 'try' at kicking for goal.

Early in the second half of the game the Scottish forwards managed to push an extended scrum over the English try line and Angus Buchanan grounded the ball, claiming the first ever international rugby try. The dispute that followed, however, set the tone for the treatment of match officials by players to this day. Referees were not introduced into the game until a few years later and so it was the job of an umpire observing proceedings from the touchline to resolve any disputes. H. H. Almond, the umpire that day, was accordingly subjected to a barrage of protestations from both sides and was called upon to decide whether the try should stand.

Having no idea whether the try had been correctly obtained or not, he confessed afterwards, 'When an umpire is in doubt, I think he is justified in deciding against the side which makes the most noise. They are probably in the wrong.' The English players were the loudest and so Scotland were awarded the try and William Cross kicked the conversion (another first for international rugby), securing the only points of the game. To this day rugby players are much more likely to quietly accept a referee's decision than those who play with the round ball.

The Scottish Football Union was founded in 1873 at the Glasgow Academy and was made up of teams from Edinburgh,

Glasgow, St Andrews and the West of Scotland. In an early hint of the independent streak that was to come, a number of Scottish clubs which had previously been members of the Rugby Football Union opted instead to affiliate to the Scottish Football Union. They didn't feel the need to use the word 'Rugby' until 1924 when they became the Scottish Rugby Union.

## BAREBACK RUGBY

Scotland's reputation for meanness when it comes to matters financial is of course entirely undeserved. It is not helped, however, by the story told by Jock Wemyss, who played as a prop forward for Scotland in the first part of the last century. In those days players were expected to bring their own shorts and club socks to matches. Only their national shirt would be provided. In 1920 Scotland were to play their first fixture against France since the Armistice at the end of the Great War and Jock, who had also played before the war, was named in the side that travelled to Parc des Princes in Paris. As he sat in the changing room, ready to play, Jock was disturbed to note the kit man pass him by when handing out the shirts. When he inquired, Jock was told that, as he had played before the war, he was supposed to have brought his old shirt. It was only when he ran out onto the pitch bare-chested, that the club officials relented and gave him a new shirt.

# WALES

An early football game played in Pembrokeshire in Wales was called 'cnapan' and would pit sides with up to 1,000 players against each other; pretty impressive, when the population of the entire country was just 587,000 in 1801. Rugby itself was introduced by the vice-principal of Lampeter College, the theologian Dr Rowland Williams, who brought the game back with him from Cambridge around 1850. Lampeter College's rugby club has been nicknamed the Mad Pilgrims in recognition of its religious roots, and also the Fighting Parsons on account of one old boy's touring side named the Old Parsons, who played in a sky-blue and white kit in memory of the historic link to Cambridge through Dr Williams.

The first international fixture wasn't arranged until 1881, when a Mr Richard Mullock, a leading light of the South Wales Football Union, took a somewhat disorganised side over to Richardson's Field in Blackheath. In scenes that modern-day lovers of the amateur game will recognise all too well, two of the Welsh players who were expected to play failed to turn up at the ground. Two bystanders with tenuous connections to Wales were cajoled into pulling on a scarlet shirt emblazoned with the Prince of Wales feathers. In what should have been a good omen, both sides gathered at the Princess of Wales pub, changed and walked the half a mile across the commons to the game. That is, the omen would have been good if it hadn't included drinking a few too many pre-match pints. The Welsh performed considerably under par and, after a couple of injuries, they were quickly back down to 13 players. In the end they lost by seven goals, six tries and a dropped goal to nothing. The English RFU were deeply unimpressed by their visitors' poor performance and they dropped the fixture the following season.

The Welsh, however, retreated to the Valleys, formed their own union and generally put their house in order. After a few years, they began to take to rugby like no other nation, totally dominating the international game in the early 1900s and going unbeaten between March 1907 and January 1910. They remained a major force in world rugby until the First World War, when the sport was suspended for four seasons. They would return to dominate again throughout the 1970s with the likes of Gareth Edwards, Barry John, Mervyn Davies, John Taylor, J. P. R. Williams, Gerald Davies and John Dawes.

# IRELAND

The Irish had a game called 'caid' involving two large teams, a leather-clad, inflated pig's bladder and quite a lot of physical contact. And with the huge quantities of beer that were consumed, it wasn't just the pig who got bladdered.

No doubt in search of the craic, a few English public schoolboys found their way to Dublin University and in 1854 formed the first Irish rugby football club. Other clubs were formed soon after and the game gradually took hold. The Irish Football Union was formed in 1874, but to the irritation of the clubs in Belfast none of their representatives were present. In a fit of pique the Ulster-based clubs went on to form their own North of Ireland Union, which made selection for the forthcoming fixture against England a little tense. Eventually, however, the two unions agreed to select ten players each to the 20-player team, though that was the full extent of their cooperation. When the players arrived at the Oval in London for the game, there was chaos. Many of them had never met before and no one had given any thought to what positions anyone would play. Backs ended up as forwards and vice versa. Two players didn't turn up at all. The visiting team were penned back into their own half for most of the game, with the Irish wit and critic of the day Jacques McCarthy writing: 'The whole lot were immaculately innocent of training.' In the end, Ireland held on to lose by just one goal, a dropped goal and a try to nil.

But in 1879 the two rugby unions came together and formed an all-Ireland union which exists to this day and has survived throughout the sectarian troubles that divided the island of Ireland. Whilst most other sports compete separately as Republic of Ireland and Northern Ireland sides, rugby somehow seems to manage to survive and thrive in spite of the religious and political differences.

Rugby even managed to navigate its way around Rule 42 of the Gaelic Athletic Association, which prohibited the playing of non-Gaelic games in GAA stadiums. An amendment was agreed to allow rugby internationals to be played in Dublin at Croke Park whilst the Lansdowne Road ground was being redeveloped.

# RUGBY OFFICIALLY BECOMES INTERNATIONAL

With the four home nations all up and running with the ball, all the elements were now in place for the establishment of one of the key identifying features of this great sport; a characteristic of the game that would last through the ages, defining the sport, establishing its brand and demonstrating clearly its fundamental values. I refer, of course, to the well-established rugby principle of all the other nations basically hating England.

Now you might have thought, especially if you are English, that the rest of the world would be grateful for having the gift of rugby bestowed upon them by a kind, warm and generous England. Well, oddly enough, things didn't turn out like that. It didn't take long for the three nations of Ireland, Scotland and Wales to find a reason to fall out with the nation that founded the game.

The initial flash point was a disputed try in the 1884 season, the first year all four of the home nations played against each other and the prospect of a first international championship title was dangled tantalisingly under their broken noses. England and Scotland had won both their games thus far and were set to decide the championship with a clash at Blackheath.

Eight thousand fans made their way to south-east London and witnessed Scotland take an early lead with an unconverted try. Then early in the second half came the incident that would shape the international game for the rest of time and establish England as the perennial bad guys. Scotland won a scrum close to their own try line but in the aftermath one of their forwards knocked the ball backwards, whereupon it was scooped up by an English forward who made a run towards the posts. A quick pass to another forward and England were over the line and claiming a try.

Now, here's where it gets complicated, so do pay attention, please. The Scots appealed against the try on the basis that their own knock-back had been against the laws. Being sticklers for that sort of thing, they wanted to be formally and appropriately punished for their transgression, and much as they would have liked to concede the try to the English, the laws were sacrosanct and needed to be enforced. The modern-day rule about playing advantage had not been established and the Scots contended that the game should have been stopped at that point, before the try had been scored. The English argued that it was perfectly acceptable for a team to knock the ball backwards and, even if it hadn't been, it seemed a bit off for the Scottish to gain from their own misdemeanour. The debate rumbled on but eventually the Irish referee George Scriven awarded the try to England. It was duly converted and England won the game.

Things didn't end there, of course, and an exchange of letters between the English and Scottish unions continued for months, arguing the finer points of the ruling. The fixture the following year was cancelled as the two sides had failed to come to an agreement. Eventually, the Irish stepped in and proposed the formation of a neutral, international body to frame the laws and arbitrate on any disputes. The English thought that was why they had set up the RFU in the first place and refused to join the new International Board. The Celtic nations went ahead and set it up anyway, leaving England out in the cold for two years. After some high-level arbitration involving the second-most senior judge in Scotland a compromise was reached and England joined the new body. International games between all four home nations resumed, but the visceral loathing of England had been firmly settled as an underlying tenet of every future game.

## AUSTRALIA

Rugby very nearly didn't happen in Australia. When young Tom Wills, aged 14, was sent from Australia to Rugby School, you might have thought he would have returned and helpfully got the game of rugby underway. But he went on to start up Australian Rules football instead. This game, developed as a way of keeping cricketers fit during the winter, is played on an oval pitch. Tom Wills wrote at the time that 'Rugby was not a game for us; we wanted a winter pastime but men could be harmed if thrown on the ground so we thought differently.'

However, rugby gradually began to be played in schools across Australia during the 1860s as teachers from England brought the Rugby School rules along with them. Scratch sides were occasionally assembled to play against visiting naval ships, and the first club was created at Sydney University. Again, things didn't get off to a great start. The *Sydney Morning Herald* reported that 'On the afternoon of 19th August, 1865 a rugby match was played on the University grounds. After an exciting struggle, which lasted an hour and a half, during which no goals were obtained by either side, the game was stopped owing to a misunderstanding with regard to the rules.'

Fortunately, though, by 1874 there were enough clubs to form the Southern Rugby Union. Initially it was administered from Twickenham in England, but in 1892 the Southern Rugby Union became the New South Wales Rugby Union and administered the sport alongside the Queensland Rugby Union.

The Australian national side is known as the Wallabies after the endearing marsupial that's not quite big enough to be a kangaroo. On their first tour to the Northern Hemisphere, some sections of the British press attempted to bestow the nickname of 'the Rabbits' on the visiting team. The Australians were not keen to have their national side named after a species that had been imported from England and had become a pest. A vote among the tourists was arranged to select a more suitable animal and the native wallaby was duly elected.

The First World War brought an abrupt halt to the development of rugby union in Australia, as it was felt by all the authorities that playing on would be inappropriate whilst so many men were fighting overseas. Rugby league, however, continued during the war and a number of players defected to the alternative code. Rugby union didn't really get going again Down Under until 1928, when the Queensland Authorities decided to pull their collective socks up.

## THE AUSTRALIAN DISPENSATION

Rugby has the Australians to thank for the creation of full backs who could run. This wasn't anything to do with their convict heritage (presumably it was the convicts who couldn't run away fast enough that were caught and deported). No, it was a law change known as the 'Australian Dispensation' that altered the way the game was played, much to the benefit of the spectator. Prior to 1968, the job of the full back was to tackle, catch the ball and hoof it straight into touch, as far up the pitch as possible. This was allowed from anywhere on the field of play and could result in some rather dull games. One fixture between Wales and Scotland in 1963 saw 111 lineouts as the Welsh full back Clive Rowlands spent the entire game kicking for touch. His side were dominating the lineout but as soon as they won the ball it would go straight to Rowlands, who would promptly kick it straight into touch again.

The Australians had been given a dispensation to vary the rules such that no one could kick the ball into touch from outside the 25-yard line. This adjustment was adopted by the rest of the world in 1968 and as an immediate result the number of tries scored by full backs soared as they focused a little more on their running game rather than always kicking for touch.

The Wallabies became a dominant world force in the 1980s with an all-conquering tour to the British Isles in 1984. In 1999 they made history by being the first nation to win the Rugby World Cup twice, beating France in the final at the Millennium Stadium in Cardiff by 35–12.

# NEW ZEALAND

In New Zealand, long before the Europeans put in an appearance, the Maoris played a game called 'ki-o-rahi' involving two teams competing on a circular pitch. The game is still played, with a small ball called a 'ki', made from woven flax. This ancient fibrous plant material also seems to have helped to weave together the DNA that would later form the all-conquering All Blacks. The Kiwis traditionally held a gathering of the players called a 'tatu' before each game of ki-o-rahi, to agree the rules that would be applied; this is in stark contrast to the rest of the world, who opted to convene committees as the most reliable way of making the laws of any game as complex and convoluted as possible so that people who couldn't play the game could at least argue about it for weeks, months, even years afterwards.

We have Christ's College in Finchley, north London, to thank for introducing New Zealand to the game of rugby. In 1867 the fee-paying boarding school welcomed a young Charles Monro from New Zealand and with a strict, highly disciplined regime began to prepare him for a military career. However, it also taught him the set of rules for football as played at Rugby School, and the young Monro played for the school's second team. When he returned to New Zealand in 1870 Monro set about convincing Nelson Football Club to try out the Rugby School rules. They played New Zealand's first rugby game on 14 May 1870 against Nelson College in front of a crowd of 200 spectators.

Old boys from English public schools established rugby clubs in Auckland, South Canterbury and Otago, and, helped by a growing transport network and legislation that led to a growing practice of half-day working on Saturdays, the game quickly caught on throughout the provinces. When Auckland played Christchurch in 1875 there were 3,000 spectators.

New Zealand are, of course, famous for their Haka. The pre-match ritual of a traditional warlike chant performed by the New Zealand national rugby team, with accompanying chest beating, thigh slapping and exaggerated facial gestures, goes back to their very first international tour. Before their own national rugby union had been formally constituted, a Maori team was assembled, packed off on a steamer and arrived at Tilbury Docks in England on 27 September 1888. Wearing traditional capes, they performed a Haka before their first game against a scratch Surrey XV, which they then went on to win 4–1.

In 1905 the first All Blacks team to tour Britain, known as 'the Originals', performed the now popular 'Ka Mate' Haka before their Welsh Test, and the *West Coast Times* reported that, 'The crowd listened and watched in pleased silence, and thundered their approval at its close.'

## STANDING UP TO THE HAKA

The Haka has not always been so popular with opposition teams obliged to stand and respectfully watch the New Zealand side pump themselves up while directing hostile gestures at them before a game. Various international sides have responded to the Haka in different ways with varying degrees of success. The Irish side of 1989 linked arms and, led by captain and lock Willie Anderson, edged forwards during the performance until they were almost nose-to-nose with the All Blacks team. In 2008 the Welsh stood motionless after the Haka, leading to a two-minute stare off with the Kiwis and ignoring the referee's pleas for them to begin the game.

Legendary Irish centre Brian O'Driscoll was accused of disrespecting the Kiwi tradition, however, when he picked up a piece of grass and threw it in the air in a gesture symbolising the picking up of a white feather. A few minutes into the Test, O'Driscoll was spear-tackled by the New Zealand captain Tana Umaga, dislocating the Irish centre's shoulder and putting him out of the game and the rest of the tour.

At Cardiff Arms Park in 1905, in response to the All Blacks' Haka, the Welsh players led the massed terraces in a powerful rendition of 'Land of My Fathers' and inspired a heroic victory over the New Zealanders. No one would suggest that the impartial referee would have been influenced by the intimidating atmosphere in the stadium, but an apparent late try by Kiwi centre Bob Deans was ruled to have been held up in a tackle and not scored. The power of pre-match Welsh voices lifted in praise of the Almighty who does, we are told, move in mysterious ways.

For all its bravado and symbolism, the intimidating chant is thought to be linked to the story of a Maori warrior, Te Rauparaha, who, running away to escape his enemies, hides in a storage pit. Emerging blinking into the sunlight he sees a friendly chief, known as Te Wharerangi ('the hairy man').

*Ka mate, ka mate*
*Ka ora, ka ora*
*Tenei te tangata puhuruhuru*
*Nana nei tiki mai whakawhiti te ra*
*A upane, kaupane*
*Upane, kaupane*
*Whiti te ra.*

These words are translated as:

*It is death, it is death*
*It is life, it is life*
*This is the hairy man*
*Who brought the sun and caused it to shine again*
*An upward step, another upward step*
*An upward step...*
*The sun shines.*

It's really not that terrifying when you think about it.

New Zealanders do not have a monopoly on pre-rugby war-dance rituals. The Tongans, Fijians and Samoans have their own Hakas to help fire up their players and intimidate the opposition. On the other hand, the English have yet to pluck up the courage to begin all their international fixtures by celebrating the traditional cultural art form that is the Morris dance. Perhaps one day?

Today the All Blacks are the most feared and respected international rugby union side; their rather appropriate motto is 'Subdue and penetrate'. As the former Australian player Phil

Kearns said, 'You can go to the end of time, the last World Cup in the history of mankind, and the All Blacks will be favourites for it.' They have now won the game's greatest prize three times, more than any other nation.

# SOUTH AFRICA

Dutch colonialists found their way to the southern tip of Africa in 1652 and, had things stayed like that, the Springboks today might have been playing korfball or formed themselves into an international clog-dancing troupe. Though late to the party, Britain established control in 1806 and the doors were open for a spot of imperialist cultural importation. The public school that got in first turned out to be Winchester College, whose old boy the Reverend George Ogilvie imposed his old school's rules, and so the Winchester Game was the variety of football played most prominently to begin with. Rugby football arrived eventually in the shape of Sir William Henry Milton, who had played for England as a back. He gradually convinced the local clubs, starting with his own, called The Villagers, to switch to the rugby code, before toddling off to go and administer some other part of the British Empire in Africa.

The young Boers from the agricultural belt rather took to the game and then the first British touring side arrived in 1891. The British captain came with a gold cup, which had been a gift from the late shipping magnate Sir Donald Currie. The trophy was to be presented to the South African team that gave them the best game during the tour. The trophy was awarded to the side from Griqualand West and was then donated to the South African

Rugby Board and became the trophy for the inter-province domestic competition. The Currie Cup is still competed for between the leading sides in South Africa to this day.

The highs and lows of rugby in South Africa have been closely linked to global politics. The team's very first tour of the Northern Hemisphere in 1906 was an attempt to improve international relations following the Boer War, while the sporting boycott during the 1980s reduced their national side to playing matches against rebel tours.

In contrast to the isolation of and hostility to South African rugby in those years, hosting the 1995 Rugby World Cup was one of the most uplifting and inclusive moments in post-apartheid South Africa and in international sport. Few will forget seeing President Nelson Mandela wearing the Springbok jersey, which up until that point had been seen as a symbol of white suppression in the country, as he handed the Webb Ellis Cup to captain Francois Pienaar.

# FRANCE

Before the British sailed over the channel with some inflated rugby balls in the hold, the French had had to make do with a leather ball filled with hay, bran or horsehair. The French version of the traditional village football game was called *la soule*, which was played on religious holidays and saints' days and at weddings, and which involved getting the ball into the opponent's goal using hands, feet or sticks.

Rugby was introduced to the French in the 1870s. In Le Havre, a group of British residents began playing a hybrid of football and rugby, and in 1877 a group of businessmen in Paris formed English Taylors RFC. Soon there were two Parisian teams, Racing Club de France and Stade Français, and by the time of the Paris Olympics in 1900 the French were sufficiently well organised to pick up the gold medal. But if it began in the north, nowadays rugby is the dominant sport in the south of France, with almost all the senior sides based in that region.

Parisian spectators, it seems, took a little longer to get their Gauloises-infused brains around the finer points of the laws of the game. The authorities took to printing the laws on the back of tickets for international games played in Paris for the general edification of the French capital's residents. They must have omitted to print the regulation concerning the unquestionable and irrefutable correctness of the referee, as, in 1913, the French crowd staged a near riot in protest at the decision of an English official, who had rather strictly applied the laws as he oversaw the French defeat to Scotland on New Year's Day. The hapless ref had to be scuttled out of the ground by a quick-thinking French winger, but so appalled were the Scots that they immediately cancelled all future fixtures against the French.

It was not until 1920 that Scotland returned to Paris. Scotland won the fixture after a much tighter game, by just one converted try to nil. As he blew the final whistle the referee looked round with horror to see the French fans rushing towards him. Though he feared a repeat of the riots from when the sides last met, fortunately on this occasion the spectators were assembling to carry the referee from the pitch at shoulder height in a gesture of Gallic goodwill and general sportsmanship. Friendly relations with the Scots were restored and both sides resumed their traditional pastime of hating the English.

The modern French side have a reputation for playing a rough, and some might say brutal, game in the forwards but combining it with a certain Gallic flair in the backs. Pierre Berbizier, the former French international scrum half and coach of Racing Metro, spoke for his nation when he said, 'If you can't take a punch you should play table tennis.' Tim Lane, the former Australian rugby coach put it slightly differently, saying, 'I think the French always niggle, grabbing blokes around the balls and the eyes and that sort of thing.'

The French national side didn't really come into its own until the late 1950s and they won the Five Nations tournament for the first time in 1959. Gloriously unpredictable, the French have made it to the World Cup final three times but have not yet managed to pick up the Webb Ellis Cup.

# ITALY

The Romans had a word for it and the word was *harpastum*. Their small-ball game involved two teams of between five and 12 players each attempting to keep a ball on their side of a rectangular pitch. Almost the exact reverse of rugby, but a format that led to a lot of familiar wresting and grappling. Julius Caesar was thought to be a big fan when he wasn't busy bewaring the Ides of March or being stabbed in the back. He saw it as a way of keeping his troops fit and battle-ready.

It wasn't until the end of the nineteenth century that the oval ball turned up, having been brought to Genoa by English trading merchants for a few games. Italian workers returning from the south of France also brought the game back with them to the Po Valley in the north of the country. Italy formed their Rugby Federation in 1928 and played their first international game in 1929, which they lost 9–0 to Spain in Barcelona.

## RUGBY AND IL DUCE

Benito Mussolini's fascist regime took a brief interest in the game, playing up the Ancient Roman connection and setting up a propaganda committee to promote the game to universities. Mussolini's office wrote to the RFU in Twickenham in 1932, asking them to organise a congress of European rugby federations to encourage the spread of the sport. Twickenham wrote back curtly dismissing the idea as 'neither workable nor desirable'. Mussolini went off and instead focused on his football team, which was doing rather well at the time. After the Second World War, though, Allied troops in Italy helped to develop the game of rugby, and an assortment of foreign players and coaches continued to support the game as it developed throughout the nation.

In the 1980s an effort to promote the game created a tax regime that made it very tempting for wealthy sponsors to invest in rugby. The fashion business Benetton set up its own team in Treviso and international-standard players with a little bit of Italian ancestry were lured in to play for the Italian top-flight sides. The national side started to strengthen and in 1987 they were invited to take part in the first ever Rugby World Cup. They have qualified for every World Cup since, but have yet to progress beyond the group stage.

Known as 'the Azzurri' ('the Blues'), the Italian rugby team had impressed enough to earn themselves a place in the Five Nations tournament in 2000, turning it into the imaginatively titled Six Nations. Although they are the perennial underdogs of the competition they are many people's second-favourite team. Their occasional victories are celebrated by all the other nations, apart obviously from the side they have just defeated. The Six Nations side they get to beat is usually Scotland: Italy won their first game in the Six Nations at home to Scotland and in 2007 they managed to secure their first away win when again they defeated Scotland at Murrayfield by 37–17.

One of Italy's greatest stars played his first two international Tests for Argentina, the country of his birth, but in 1991 Diego Domínguez returned to his mother's homeland and began playing for the Azzurri. Over a glorious career he won a further 73 caps and remains one of only five players in history (the others being Dan Carter, Jonny Wilkinson, Neil Jenkins and Ronan O'Gara) to score more than 1,000 international points.

## ARGENTINA

Rugby travelled to Argentina with British immigrants in the mid-nineteenth century, although for a while they rather kept the game to themselves and their exclusive native-free clubs. Over time, though, the game has expanded its appeal to wider Argentinian society beyond the expat elite.

## RUGBY AND CHE GUEVARA

One of the very first people to write about rugby in Argentina was the young Che Guevara. Though better known for his revolutionary rather than rugby-playing skills, Che was passionate about the game and an accomplished inside centre. Born in Buenos Aires, he suffered from chronic asthma and was sent by his father to a town in the foothills of the Sierras Chicas in the centre of Argentina for some clean air and healthy living. It was there in 1942 that he discovered rugby, dashing off the pitch every 20 minutes or so to use a rather primitive inhaler and keep his asthma at bay.

After secondary school he returned to Buenos Aires and played for three different clubs and published a rugby magazine called *Tackle*. It was in that publication that he first began to write about some of the social iniquities in Argentinian society, articles which earned him a visit from local police not terribly well disposed to his communist leanings. It was then, with a rugby-playing mate, Alberto Granado, that he set off on his famous motorcycle tour of South America, which in turn led to a meeting with Fidel Castro and a walk-on part in the Cuban Revolution. How very different so many of those T-shirts and student-bedroom posters would have looked if the iconic photograph of the great revolutionary had shown him in a scrum cap rather than the more familiar revolutionary beret.

Politics and rugby have often clashed in Argentina. After one game in 1890, all 30 players and the entire crowd of 2,500 supporters were jailed by police who suspected that the whole event had been a front for a political meeting.

In rugby circles, Argentina is often described as the Italy of South America and, like Italy, it has rather taken to rugby in the modern era, becoming another popular international rugby underdog. Admitted to the Southern Hemisphere's Rugby Championship in 2012, playing against New Zealand, Australia and South Africa, its occasional victories are celebrated widely. Strengthened by playing such robust opposition on a regular basis, Argentina has done rather better than Italy in World Cups, making the semi-finals in 2007 and 2015. However, within Argentina the game remains largely amateur, so for many years most of the senior international players relocated overseas to play for professional sides in Europe. But a new ruling in 2016 may transform the Argentinian game, as in order to be eligible for international selection players now have to compete in their domestic Super Rugby league.

# PAPUA NEW GUINEA

When Australia took over administering Papua New Guinea after the Second World War, the Australians who travelled there happened to take rugby league rather than union with them. By the 1960s the game had completely taken hold of the nation. With a population of just seven million, Papua New Guinea is the only nation to declare rugby league as its national sport. Matches in Papua New Guinea are a huge event and spectators have been known to walk for days in full tribal dress to attend fixtures.

There are 600 different languages spoken in Papua New Guinea and tribal disputes can occasionally make team management tricky. During one tour, the organisers had to work hard to keep the news from two players that their respective tribes had gone to war.

Close links have been formed between Papua New Guinea and the English rugby league side Hull Kingston Rovers. In 1996 Hull KR signed Papua New Guinean star John Okul and his friend Stanley Gene. Gene went on to coach at the Hull KR academy and Gateshead Thunder, as well as serving as head coach for his nation in 2010. There is a Facebook page linking supporters from Hull KR and those from Papua New Guinea, which at the time of writing had over 9,000 likes and supporters swapping team kit and news about their players through the social-media site.

# FIJI

The tiny group of South Pacific islands that make up the nation of Fiji has a population of only 880,000 but as many as 560 rugby clubs. Rugby is the national sport and was introduced by English and New Zealanders to the Fijian Soldiers of the Native Constabulary. Whilst their 15-a-side team is a very respectable second-tier nation, and has made the quarter-finals of the Rugby World Cup on two occasions, it is the sevens side who are world beaters. Quite a bit of their success has been attributed to one Ben Ryan, a more recent English export. Ben took over coaching the Fijian sevens side, having fallen out of favour at Twickenham where he had been responsible for the English sevens team for six years. Within a month and a half he found himself in the tiny island state of Fiji and winning instant celebrity status.

Describing himself as a '44-year-old ginger bloke with glasses', Ryan stands out a little among the locals and, as a result, is mobbed wherever he goes. A typical day out in the city will see him being asked for hundreds of photographs as everyone knows who he is. 'I get mobbed like I am Brad Pitt whenever I step out of the house,' he told *Telegraph Sport*.

Ryan took the sevens team to success in the World Sevens Series, sealing the title in London in May 2015. Fiji had an unofficial national holiday the day after their side qualified for the Rio Olympics and from there the pressure on Ryan built up to such a degree that the Prime Minister told him, only half-jokingly, not to bother coming back to Fiji without the Olympic gold medal. He needn't have worried. Fiji were triumphant in Rio, winning the gold in style and pulverising Great Britain in the final by 43 points to 7.

## WHY ARE PACIFIC ISLANDERS SO GOOD AT RUGBY?

Analysis by *The Economist* in 2016 came up with three main reasons:

- Enthusiasm – There are an estimated 180,000 Fijian men aged between 14 and 40, and 155,000 of them play rugby.

- Cohesion – Rugby brings an otherwise divided nation together. In 2006 a military coup was allegedly post poned until after a big game. The teams sing together, perform tribal dances together and pray together.

- Science – A paper from the University of the Sunshine Coast, published in the *Journal of Sports Sciences* in January 2015, reported that elite Polynesian rugby athletes have different distribution patterns of fat mass and lean mass compared to Caucasians, which may influence their suitability for particular positions. The research suggested that Polynesians are heavier, have more muscular limbs and are able to generate 'greater force in explosive movements' than players of other ethnicities.

# JAPAN

The international journey of rugby from the playing fields of the English public schools to every corner of the globe seemed to be complete when Japan secured an earth-shattering victory over South Africa in the 2015 Rugby World Cup.

Japan, previously ranked thirteenth in the world, had only ever won one World Cup match before and were not expected to beat the Springboks when they met in Brighton for their group match. They had recruited the former Australian coach Eddie Jones, who had steadily and quietly transformed the 'Brave Blossoms' into a side that had the wherewithal to compete with the very best in the game. Japan started the game brightly but after 33 minutes South Africa were 12–10 ahead and everyone expected that they would begin to assert their dominance and secure a solid win. Japan, however, had other ideas and as South Africa scored tries Japan collected penalties and scored a try of their own.

Going into the final minutes Japan were just three points behind and, after a sustained period of pressure from their forwards, won a penalty just five metres from the posts. Kicking the penalty would secure three points and a very respectable draw, but as one commentator said at the time, a draw is a bit like kissing your sister, and the Japanese captain opted instead for a scrum and the chance of a glorious win. The scrum wheeled and buckled and collapsed, but after three attempts the ball eventually emerged and a few phases of play later Japan were over the line creating one of the greatest upsets in the history of the game.

# REST OF THE WORLD

Rugby has grown to be one of the world's great sports. At the time of writing there are 120 rugby unions in different nations around the world; 102 national teams compete against each other and are ranked by the International Rugby Board. New Zealand on one side of the globe sits proudly at the top of those rankings for most of the time; its lowest ever ranking has been third. Meanwhile, at the bottom of the rankings, a few sides had their ranking points halved in January 2015 for not having played a game in the previous 12 months. Just above that little batch sits Finland, who, in spite of having a climate that leaves their pitches frozen solid for much of the year, still manage to get out an international side, play some fixtures, lose most of them gallantly and celebrate with several bottles of vodka until the sun goes down. Here are some lesser-known facts relating to the unsung nations of world rugby:

- The tiny island nation of **Vanuatu** holds the record for the most Rugby World Cup matches played without winning a single game. They have scored 40 points, but in just five games have also conceded 246.

- **Paraguay** holds the record for the largest margin of defeat in an international fixture after losing to Argentina 152–0 in May 2002.

- **Chinese Taipei** did manage to do slightly better, collecting three points in a game against Japan, also in 2002, which made their opponents' 155 points somewhat easier to bear.

- **Samoa** played their first matches with empty coconut shells, until the New Zealand Rugby Union gave them a few balls in the early 1900s. Their international fixture against Tonga in 1924 was very nearly not reported in the *Samoa Times* because the rugby correspondent was at a hopscotch match instead. Fortunately one of the newspaper's compositors attended the rugby and reported that the score, which was then displayed using notches carved into a nearby tree, was 14–5 to Tonga.

## THE BARBARIANS

Often playing around the fringes of international competitions, there is one multinational rugby club that defies normal sporting conventions and is more than a match for any national side. Formed in 1890 by William Percy Carpmael, the Barbarians were a side with no ground and no clubhouse. Membership was by invitation and the only qualification was that the player had to be of a high enough standard on the pitch and a decent chap off it. The dream was for the Barbarians to be an utterly cosmopolitan side spreading good fellowship among rugby players.

The Barbarians' early tours were around the UK, but in 1948 they were invited by the Home Nations to put together a side to play the visiting Australians. The Australians were keen to secure some additional gate receipts in order to fund an extension to their tour to play in Canada. The game, which the Barbarians won 9–6, proved to be such a success that a match against the Barbarians has been a highlight of subsequent tours ever since.

With players drawn from all over the world, the Barbarians have beaten all of the leading Southern Hemisphere sides at one time or another and enjoyed fixtures against the Home Nations, the British and Irish Lions and some of the lower-ranked rugby nations such as Tunisia, Germany and Belgium. They pride themselves in playing open, free-running rugby and are always a delight to watch.

## BARBARIANS FACT FILE

- Players from 25 different countries have turned out for the Barbarians since 1890.

- The Barbarians arguably scored the best ever try, against the All Blacks in 1973, when the ball was carried from inside the Barbarians' 25-yard line, through seven pairs of hands, before Gareth Edwards scored under the posts.

- Tony O'Reilly of Old Belvedere and Ireland played 30 times for the club between 1955 and 1962, scoring a club record of 38 tries.

- The Barbarians' first tour consisted of games against Huddersfield and Bradford.

- There is no such country as Barbaria.

# LEGENDS XV

. . . . . . . . . . . . . . . . . . . . . . . . . . . . . . . . . . . . . . . . . .

Perhaps one of the simplest ways to express and share what it is that makes us love rugby is to take each position one by one and choose a single player in that position who has captured and embodied what is great about the game. Everyone who loves rugby would have a slightly different list, the point being that we all do have a list. And anyone who knows the game would agree that there is something about each position that attracts a certain sort of personality, a certain breed, a certain character. So here, for your consideration and review, are the 15 players who often come to mind first when we think about the position they play in or played.

## ❶ ADAM JONES

For the love of rugby, I would always want to have Welsh tighthead prop **Adam Jones** in any Legends side I was creating. Christened Cro-Magnon Man by Boris Johnson, London's former mayor and subsequent British foreign secretary, in a perfect example of a pot calling a kettle black, Jones has a tangled mop of dark curly hair that, drenched in sweat, sticks to his face along with anything and everything else. Placing your head and neck in the front row of a scrum is an unpleasant enough experience as it is, but to have to do it with the added risk of getting caught up in the Welshman's Medusa-like tresses must make the entire prospect even more daunting. More than just his hair, of course, Jones has an impressive record and is one of only a handful of players to have won three Grand Slams with Wales, in 2005, 2007 and 2012.

During Jones's early career concerns about his fitness meant that he would normally be substituted fairly early in a game, but fitness is never really a top priority for the front row. Jones's job, along with any front-row player, is to absorb in his neck, shoulders, back and legs the enormous pressure of two great packs coming together, whilst remaining tactically astute enough to secure a minor advantage with the slightest tweak to your stance and binding, all under the close scrutiny of a watchful referee. Maybe his flowing locks distract the referees too, allowing him to practise the dark arts of the scrum in an even darker way, but something about him and his 95 international caps makes him first on my Legends XV team sheet.

## ❷ BRIAN MOORE

For the position of hooker, I am more conflicted. I am tempted to call up Hika Reid, the New Zealander who played nine Tests for the All Blacks in the 1980s, but only so that I can give the commentator the pleasure of pointing him out, as Bill McLaren did with some relish, as 'Hika the hooker from Ngongotaha'. But for me the number two shirt has to go to **Brian Moore**, England's hooker from 1987 to 1995. Nicknamed Pitbull, he has described himself as an uneven, cynical and sometimes over-intense character, but you can forgive him all of that as he seemed to have an uncanny knack of winding up the opposition and drawing infringements and penalties out of them. He was a master of the mind games that go on between international sides and was just what you need in the middle of your front row.

Brian Moore was born in 1961 and was brought up by adoptive parents in Halifax, West Yorkshire. A grammar school boy, he went on to get a law degree in Nottingham and practised as a lawyer throughout his rugby career. He would quote Shakespeare speeches in the changing room before big games and preferred a glass of wine to the rugby player's more traditional post-match pint of beer. After his rugby career he became wine correspondent for the *Today* newspaper and then *The Sun*.

In one celebrated game against France in Paris in 1991 he was reported to have so wound up Serge Blanco that the Frenchman lashed out and knocked out the much more diminutive back Nigel Heslop. Speaking after the game, Moore said, 'There's two types of hardness. There's the bloke who punches someone from behind like they did today and other people who take it and get on with the game. We took it, we got on with the game and we got the penalties, and that's fair enough.'

## ❸ JASON LEONARD

At loose-head prop we are calling up **Jason Leonard**, England's most capped player with 114 international appearances. He earned his nickname as the 'Fun Bus' on an England tour to South Africa in 1994 when, as a result of an injury sustained at the end of the domestic season, he wasn't quite as fighting fit as the rest of the squad and was carrying a few more pounds than usual. The bright-red England training top was usually a baggy cotton number but on this occasion it was looking rather skintight on Leonard. Fellow player Martin Bayfield declared that cockney Leonard looked like a big red London bus and the name stuck.

Jason Leonard played an integral role in England's World Cup victory in 2003, coming on as a substitute in the eightieth minute (there was extra time to be played) to stabilise an English scrum that was incurring too many penalties. He introduced himself to the referee as the most experienced front-row forward in the world and said, 'You know me. I'll go forwards and I'll go backwards but I won't go up and I won't go down.' The referee seemed happy enough with that and the scrums began to settle down, allowing England to play and eventually win the game.

Leonard is now President of the RFU and in demand as an after-dinner speaker. In one question and answer session, a popular format in the corporate entertainment world, Leonard was asked to comment on the future prospects for English rugby after a poor run of results. More of a cockney geezer than your classically educated public schoolboy type, Leonard nonetheless grasped for a suitably sophisticated metaphor for his well-heeled and erudite audience. He declared that England would soon rise again from the ashes 'just like a ... pheasant'. Once his Greek mythological reference had been corrected by his host, Leonard explained that he knew all along that it was 'some posh bird that began with an F'.

# ❹ RICHIE GRAY

Now, in the second row there are plenty to choose from, but in any game when Scotland are playing my eye is always drawn to the impressive **Richie Gray**, though that is mostly because he is so tall and, to top it all, has a dyed blonde mop of hair blowing about in the rarefied air to be found up at that altitude. Gray is so tall that he has to have custom-made mattresses and complains about getting cold feet in hotel beds on any tour. As a child, Gray was more of a footballer but a move to the exclusive and independent Kelvinside Academy in Glasgow found him in an environment where rugby was the only game. Initially, he didn't take to the game particularly well, telling *The Scottish Sun*, 'I was a total beanpole at school and for my first game I had to wear this big baggy shirt. It was wet and muddy with these guys charging at you. I thought it was brutal at first.' He has now played for Scotland in every age group from under-17 to the senior side, winning his first full international cap in the 2010 Six Nations against France. He was one of the few Scots considered worthy of inclusion in the Lions tour to Australia of 2013 but is head and shoulders above the rest when it comes to selection for our *For The Love of Rugby* Legends XV.

# ❺ WILLIE JOHN McBRIDE

Alongside Richie Gray, courtesy of our very own rugby time machine, is the Irish, pipe-smoking lock forward **Willie John McBride**, brought back from the 1970s when rugby was possibly at its best. McBride is there to lead the pack from an era when the physical confrontation in the forwards was a little more brutal and less regulated than it is today.

Born in County Antrim, McBride grew up on a farm. His father died when he was four and a half and his mother raised him and his siblings on her own, setting them all different jobs on the farm. As he would say later, 'When you are working on a farm, there's no such thing as stopping at half time,' so a combination of genes and environment made McBride a tall and strong child. On his first day at school the teachers were convinced that there was a mistake on the birth certificate and he should have been starting his education a year or two earlier. He first picked up a rugby ball aged 17 at the Ballymena Academy and by the age of 21 he had made his debut for Ireland against England. He would go on to play for his country 63 times.

McBride was picked for three British and Irish Lions tours but as all of them ended in defeat, he announced that he would not travel on the next tour to New Zealand in 1971. Carwyn James, the Lions coach, flew to Belfast to meet him, looked him in the eye and said, 'But Willie John, I need you.' No one had ever said that to McBride before, so he relented, warning his fellow tourists that they would face a mighty onslaught from the All Blacks and would have to be the ones not to break. During the very first game fellow Irish international Sean Lynch turned to him and said, 'You warned us about this but would somebody please count them, because I've tackled 37 of them.' The Lions, however, didn't break and went on to win the series for the first and only time on New Zealand soil.

The next Lions tour three years later was more controversial and is the one for which Willie John McBride is most remembered. The 1974 tour was to South Africa in the face of considerable political opposition and in direct contravention of the sporting boycott against the apartheid regime. McBride, no stranger to political controversy, had lived with death threats as captain of the all-Ireland side in the aftermath of Bloody Sunday. He was determined to travel to South Africa and was made tour captain. Again the Lions faced an intensely physical opposition from a side with a reputation for what is euphemistically known as off-the-ball play. McBride invented the '99' call, which, far from an indication that the team wanted Mr Whippy ice creams with a chocolate flake, was a call for every player to step in, physically confront and ideally punch the nearest Springbok. In the days before instant replays, the theory was that the referee wouldn't be able to see everything and in any case would be very unlikely to send off the entire team. After the call was used, there was some debate in the dressing room as to whether the diminutive Welsh fly half Phil Bennett had taken his responsibilities seriously, and when questioned by McBride he replied, 'I gave the ball boy a hell of a hiding.'

The Lions ended the tour undefeated, earning the nickname 'the Invincibles', and their captain, Willie John McBride, earned his place in our Legends XV.

# ❻ RICHIE McCAW

It would be churlish to leave All Black **Richie McCaw** out of the back row of any international Legends XV. The most capped international player of all time, he became captain of New Zealand in 2006 and led the team to win two consecutive World Cups in 2011 and 2015. However, he is not universally popular and even as I write this I can hear the voices of respected commentators of the game, notably the finest sporting specimens that my own Warlingham Rugby Club bar has to offer, frothing over their beer that McCaw is an incorrigible cheating Kiwi, or something even less charitable. The Australians have taken a particular dislike to him. Richie was thought to have been offside so often that #handsoffblack7 would often trend on Twitter when he played in international fixtures between the two sides. There is even an Aussie saying/T-shirt slogan/Facebook group that is used to celebrate excessive drinking – 'I'm not an alcoholic, I just drink whenever Richie McCaw is offside.' Well, that kind of is the point. The whole thing about playing in the back row, and in particular as an open-side flanker, is that it is your job early on to establish what sort of referee you are playing against and exactly how far you can go and still remain within their interpretation of the rules. McCaw does that in every game and adapts his play accordingly. He makes a point of speaking to each referee before every game to find out how they will police the rucks and mauls, the phrases that they will use and the things that they will look out for in particular. As an old experienced back-row club player once said to me, the best way to succeed in rugby is to 'cheat until you get caught'. McCaw did that successfully throughout each of his 148 international caps and probably most of his domestic games as well.

# ❼ MAGGIE ALPHONSI

One minor setback in Richie McCaw's glittering career was in 2011 when he failed to win the coveted Rugby Union Writers' Club Pat Marshall Award in spite of having just led his side to victory in the Rugby World Cup. On this occasion the prestigious trophy went to **Maggie Alphonsi,** the first woman to win the award. 'Maggie the Machine' was for many years the star player in the England women's rugby set-up. The 5 ft 4 in. Saracens flanker won 74 international caps, scored 28 tries and built a reputation for rib-crunching tackles. This was all in spite of having been born with a club foot that led to five torn hamstrings and severely restricted the amount of training, particularly running, that she could do. Brought up by her single Nigerian mother on a north London council estate, Maggie described herself as a 'bad kid – out of lessons more often than in'. Although her mother had hoped she would become a lawyer or doctor, a PE teacher at her school suggested rugby. Alphonsi caught the W6 bus to Saracens Rugby Club and has never looked back. She became captain of Saracens and with them won the women's rugby Premiership for four consecutive seasons.

There are 18,000 women now playing rugby regularly in England and many will have been inspired by Maggie the Machine. In 2011 she was voted 'The Sunday Times Sportswoman of the Year' and in 2014 she was a crucial member of the team that won the Rugby World Cup and got crowned the BBC Sports Personality Team of the Year. Aside from her appearance in our Legends XV, Maggie the Machine has now retired from the game. She briefly flirted with the idea of becoming Maggie the shot putter, contemplating a bid for the 2016 Olympic places, but found the lack of team spirit and the need to bulk up all rather off-putting. Instead, she has become Maggie the Pundit, offering expert analysis on both the men's and women's games from the relative safety of a media sofa.

# ⑧ DEAN RICHARDS

**Dean Richards** takes our number 8 slot mostly because I remember watching rugby on the television with my Dad back in the nineties, and both of us admired how this lumbering presence, with his battered face, cauliflower ears and rolled-down socks, would dominate both sets of forwards from his position at the back of the England scrum. During an era when England were transformed from the whipping boys of international rugby into winners, he won 48 England caps and was picked six times for Lions Test sides in their 1989 and 1993 tours. Playing at the end of the amateur era, Deano was a policeman for the Leicestershire Constabulary, but it was for reasons other than his professional demeanour and legal powers that he was described by England captain Will Carling as 'a good guy to have with you in a fight'.

As a coach for Harlequins, Richards was unfortunately associated with the 'Bloodgate' scandal, of which more later, but the best story that sums up why those of a certain generation who love rugby also love Dean Richards derives from some post-match antics after a dismal, try-less Five Nations game against Scotland in 1988. The game had been a frustrating, stop–start affair with the only points coming from two penalty kicks for each side and one drop goal for England. After the game there was still the formal dinner to be endured and the players made the most of the bottles of whisky that had been placed on each table. Richards teamed up with an old pal on the Scottish team, John Jeffrey, and in an effort to restore a little good humour to the occasion the two of them got hold of the Calcutta Cup. Now, this was and remains one of the most treasured and revered trophies in the game. A gift from the Calcutta Rugby Club dating back to the 1800s, the trophy was crafted from melted-down silver rupees. Pausing first to use the cup to pour champagne in the face of England hooker Brian Moore, the pair then set off into the Edinburgh night. They were later seen crossing the Waverley Bridge passing the trophy to each other as if it were a rugby ball. Neither player was known as a great ball handler when they were sober, so the trophy got somewhat battered. Naturally, the Scottish Rugby authorities were not best amused and proceeded to ban John Jeffrey from rugby for five months. Richards, however, was given a more lenient one-match ban and a rap on the knuckles. There was no permanent damage to the trophy, which was duly restored by Hamilton and Inches, one of Edinburgh's finest jewellers, who waived their £1,500 repair bill as they got such good publicity from the work and didn't want to further add to the guilt and embarrassment suffered by the players. Dean Richards went on to pick up several winners' cups with England, the Lions and Leicester without dropping too many more, so we can safely put him in charge of our Legends XV trophy cabinet.

# ⑨ GARETH EDWARDS

We are going to offer **Gareth Edwards** our number 9 shirt, which no doubt he will treasure alongside his knighthood, MBE, CBE, 53 consecutive Welsh caps, three Grand Slams and the general acknowledgement that he scored the best try ever. Edwards was the son of a miner and grew up in a small village just north of Swansea in south-west Wales, where he would play a bit of rugby and a bit of football with his friends. Indeed, he very nearly became a professional footballer, signing a professional contract with Swansea Town when he was 16. Fortunately for rugby, however, he had also been taken under the wing of a PE teacher called Bill Samuels who recognised his ability at rugby and encouraged him to apply for a scholarship to the exclusive independent Millfield School in Somerset. So one of the major English public schools can claim to have added the finishing touches to one of Wales's greatest ever players.

As a young boy Gareth Edwards used to admire and look up to Welsh international fly half Cliff Morgan, who was later to deliver the TV commentary when Edwards scored that best ever try. It came when Edwards was playing for the Barbarians against New Zealand in 1973. When the Baa-Baas lined up at Cardiff Arms Park against an All Blacks side that had been touring for three months, the feeling in the traditionally underprepared, celebrity-packed invitation side was one of nervous anticipation.

'We went on the field determined to try to win the game but petrified that we might get run over,' said Gareth Edwards. After just a few minutes of frantic kicking and a series of unpunished high tackles, Phil Bennett caught a New Zealand kick a few yards from his own try line. Edwards was at this point relieved and fully expected Bennett to kick to touch and give the side a chance to catch their breath. Bennett, however, had other ideas. He sidestepped three All Blacks and began the sequence that led to one of rugby's greatest ever moments.

The ball passed through the hands of some of the greatest players of the time – J. P. R. Williams and on to Derek Quinnell, whose burst of speed made the try possible.

Edwards, at this point, thought to himself, 'Well, I'd better follow them to see what happens,' not really expecting the play to continue for very long. It is very much the scrum half's job to chase the ball around the pitch, being ready behind every breakdown to keep his team's momentum up. Edwards was a master at this and on this occasion he was about 10 to 15 yards behind the ball. So when he eventually caught up with the play he was travelling at quite a pace, with enough momentum to pass outside the remaining New Zealand defender to score in the left corner.

Cliff Morgan captured the moment perfectly: 'This is Gareth Edwards, a dramatic start, what a score. Oooh, that fellow Edwards…' and, when he'd caught his breath, continued, 'If the greatest writer of the written word would have written that story, no one would have believed it. That really was something.' The final score was Barbarians 23, All Blacks 11.

# ⑩ JONNY WILKINSON

Naturally we will have **Jonny Wilkinson** as our fly half. It goes without saying really. He won the affection of the entire English nation and the respect of the rest of the world when his drop goal won the Rugby World Cup for England against Australia in 2003. Rugby has a place for every sort of personality and fly half was always just the right place for this quiet, shy, thoughtful and polite young man from Surrey. He began his professional rugby career for Newcastle Falcons at the age of 18. Being young and a long way from home he had to phone his mum to find out whether he needed to take his passport with him to the supermarket in order to pay by cheque for his groceries. In the same season he made his debut for England. It was his dedicated and constant training, practising his kicking for hours every day, that underpinned not only his brilliantly accurate kicking but an impressive tackling record, all of which made him the first choice for the number 10 shirt as England coach Clive Woodward prepared his side to win rugby's ultimate prize.

Jonny found the pressure of the fame that came his way quite difficult to cope with. When he returned to rugby in 2008 after a bout of injury he arrived with a new mop of wavy golden hair. He was also sporting a new understanding of quantum physics, a rudimentary grasp of Buddhism and an unfamiliar smile. The England fly half claimed in an interview with *The Times* to have come to see the world in an entirely new light, free from his worries about life, death and rugby.

While studying quantum physics, he had come across the phenomenon known as Schrödinger's Cat, whereby Austrian physicist Erwin Schrödinger used a fictitious feline in a box to explain a problem at the heart of quantum physics. In a nutshell, he claimed that a cat in a sealed box is both alive and dead until you open the box, when it is revealed to be either alive or dead.

This apparently had a huge effect on the young Wilkinson, who said. 'The idea that an observer can change the world just by looking at it… it hit me like a steam train.' He concluded that his own way of thinking about things was influencing the way they turned out. He found Buddhism helped him overcome his fear of failure and then he grew his hair a bit – as you do.

Whether it improved his rugby or lengthened his playing career as well as his hair is anyone's guess. However, if it seemed to stop him looking so stressed and miserable all the time, we can put that down to an Austrian physicist's imaginary moggie.

*The observant and numerate among you will notice that the numbers now go slightly out of order. For the love of rugby, I have no idea why the numbering doesn't follow in the order that the ball is normally passed down the line from the fly half to the centres. Perhaps it just looks a little tidier when set out on the changing room white board when the coach is sketching out the pre-match tactics. Perhaps it is just to lull one of the wingers into thinking that they might get the ball a little earlier once in a while. Either way, wingers are always 11 and 14 and centres are 12 and 13. That's just how it is.*

# ⑫ BRIAN O'DRISCOLL

When **Brian O'Driscoll** was dropped from the Lions Test side for the final game in what was to be the Irish centre's last ever

Lions tour, there were demonstrations in the streets back in his hometown. Such was the respect that he had built up over his career, which included 133 caps for Ireland, winning two Six Nations championships including one Grand Slam, and being selected for four Lions tours. So he can perhaps gain some comfort from knowing that he has been picked for our Legends XV.

He was a late developer and much smaller than other children his own age when he was growing up and discovering rugby at Blackrock College in Dublin, a hotbed of Irish schoolboy rugby. He speculated that his early pace might have been something to do with being extremely keen not to get tackled by substantially bigger boys.

When he was first introduced to the Irish international squad, the captain and hooker Keith Wood was initially unimpressed by what he later described as 'a spotty kid with glasses like coke bottles. The furthest thing from a rugby player I'd ever seen.' However, once the young man stepped onto the training pitch Wood very quickly revised his opinion. 'The guy was awesome. Everything he did seemed to be at 100 miles an hour and incredibly accurate.'

At the time Irish rugby was struggling to compete internationally in the new professional age, and the national team had a reputation as a side that ran out of steam after 50 minutes. O'Driscoll burst onto the scene by scoring a hat-trick against France in Paris in 2000, helping his side to their first victory in the French capital since 1972. The young centre was shocked by the reaction of the Irish public, reflecting later, 'It was essentially just a win, one game, but the country went nuts.'

O'Driscoll made himself very popular among his fellow Lions tourists by beating up the deeply irritating English scrum half Austin Healey in an impromptu boxing match in between games on the 2001 tour of Australia. The bout had been provoked by Healey's goading of Ronan O'Gara, who was recovering from a particularly vicious beating he had taken playing against one of the Australian sides. O'Driscoll pulled on some gloves and, much to the delight of the rest of the squad, discovering he had a bit of a knack for the pugilistic arts, put Healey firmly back in his place.

# ⑬ JEREMY GUSCOTT

The outside centre position goes to **Jeremy Guscott,** the better half of England's centre partnership of the early nineties. Whilst Will Carling was concentrating on being a very young England captain and trying to distract people from the fact that his chin looked like a bottom, Jeremy Guscott was busy scoring tries, 30 of them to be precise, and helping England on their way to four Six Nations trophies including three Grand Slams.

Born in Bath, the son of a hospital porter, Guscott was working as an apprentice bricklayer as he began his senior rugby career towards the end of the amateur era. He played for his home city from the age of seven and was spotted and signed up by the Lions selectors for the tour of Australia before he had even pulled on an England shirt. He scored a hat-trick of tries on his England debut against Romania and then went on to earn the respect of Lions tourists Down Under with a crucial grubber kick and chase at an electric pace that led to him scoring the try that won the second Test and rescued the series. As one onlooker said at the time, 'That boy will never lay another brick again.' Back in Bath his father, who had been watching the game on the television, went home, picked up a sledgehammer and knocked down a wall of the house to celebrate. Fortunately it had been due for demolition as part of a home improvement plan, but nonetheless it is a good example of the strange things that people do for the love of rugby.

## ⑪ JASON ROBINSON

For some pace on the wing we will call up **Jason Robinson**, one of the first batch of players to make the shift from league to union when the latter turned professional. Nicknamed Billy Whizz, he made his name in the Wigan Rugby League Challenge Cup winning side of 1993. He also played on the wing for the Great Britain rugby league side against New Zealand aged just 19.

As rugby league moved to become a summer sport, Robinson opted for a few games with newly professional union side Bath in the 1996 season. He continued playing league during the warmer months.

In 2000, he moved to union full time, signing for Sale Sharks and working his way into the England national team by February of the following year. He played in 56 internationals and scored 30 tries, including a memorable one in England's World Cup final victory against Australia in 2003.

He played his last international against South Africa in the World Cup final of 2007. He became head coach of Sale in 2009 but the stresses and strains of running a Premiership side didn't seem to suit him. A year later he came out of retirement to play for the National Two North side Fylde, who, oddly enough, won the league that year.

# ⑭ JONAH LOMU

On the other wing, of course, we will have the late, great **Jonah Lomu,** one of the world's first international rugby icons and possibly the best ever back. Lomu was raised in Tonga for the first six years of his life. He had a turbulent upbringing and left home at 14, when he had finally had enough of his violent and alcoholic father.

At 19 years and 45 days old he became the youngest ever All Black, winning his first cap against France in 1994. But it was in the 1995 World Cup that he really made his mark, scoring seven tries in five games. He introduced the international audience to his 'Maori sidestep'. This is where a player from a Pacific Island nation runs in a completely straight line, using their additional weight and momentum to blast away any player in their path. Lomu famously used this as he ran through England's full back Mick Catt to score one of his four tries against England in the semi-final.

His stature and strength were unusual for someone in his position on the pitch. The former All Black lock Colin Meads put it well when he said, 'I've seen a lot people like him, but they weren't playing on the wing.'

What people didn't know at the time was that Lomu was suffering from a severe kidney disorder throughout the tournament and spent most of the time between matches recovering in bed.

He had a kidney transplant in 2004, with the replacement kidney being donated by New Zealand Radio host Grant Kereama.

He played 63 times for his country between 1994 and 2002, scoring 185 points in total. His pace, power and reputation intimidated opposition defenders. If he wasn't scoring tries himself, his mere presence would create defensive gaps for his teammates to exploit. Interviewed in the *Daily Telegraph*, he said:

*When I play at my peak I get into a different zone. I become a completely different person. I can't really explain it. It's almost like you're running, but you're watching yourself while you're running – like an out-of-body experience. I do what I've got to do to get to where I need to get. You do see Mike Catt in front of you... but that's what rugby is all about. If someone is in front of you and you have to go over the top of them, that's the way the game goes.*

Jonah Lomu retired from professional rugby in 2007 but continued to be an ambassador for the game. He was working on promotional activities for the Rugby World Cup right up until his death on 18 November 2015 of a heart attack caused by his kidney disease. Some 8,000 people gathered for his funeral in Eden Park Stadium, and scores of mourners filed onto the pitch to perform a memorial Haka in his honour.

# ⑮ SERGE BLANCO

And finally, at full back, leaning on the posts smoking a Gauloise, we will have the Frenchman **Serge Blanco**. Born with

Basque and Venezuelan heritage, he grew up in south-west France and was fortunate enough to be playing rugby at a time when it was possible to combine an international career with a 40-a-day smoking habit. He still holds the record for the most international tries scored by a Frenchman – 38 in 93 Tests. After a career which included two Grand Slams, in 1981 and 1987, in what was then the Five Nations, he retired to run hotels and a sportswear brand and become president of Biarritz Olympique rugby club.

Blanco also brings a little romance to our side. It was he who said, 'Rugby is like love. You have to give before you can take. And when you have the ball it's like making love – you must think of the other's pleasure before your own.' That's just the sort of phrase that you can think up when you have all that time on your hands playing at full back and waiting for those very rare occasions when the ball comes anywhere near you.

# RUGBY IS FOR GIRLS

> **ᶠᶠ** *Everybody thinks we should have moustaches and hairy arses, but in fact you could put us all on the cover of* Vogue. **ᴶᴶ**
>
> **HELEN KIRK, WOMEN'S RUGBY PIONEER**

Whilst rugby has traditionally been seen as a more or less exclusively male sport, it is clear that a huge focus of the game's administrators around the world is to increase participation by women. In 2015, 370,000 girls took part in Get into Rugby programmes supported by World Rugby. The English RFU has awarded professional contracts to its leading female international players and other nations around the world are slowly taking similar steps. The Rio Olympics saw women's and men's sevens rugby given equal billing, and both tournaments created the same levels of drama, spectacle and athleticism. Rugby is now firmly established as a game for girls and women as well as men and boys.

Women's rugby is played in exactly the same way, on the same-size pitches, with exactly the same rules. Careful inspection of the protective layers available might reveal a slightly different distribution of the padding, but otherwise it is the same sport. Boys and girls play mini rugby together up until the age of 11, and many clubs around the country have successful women's sides. All the major international tournaments have an equivalent women's version. There is a Women's Six Nations and a Women's Rugby World Cup, and the support and media interest in the games has grown steadily over the last two decades.

In an interview with *The Observer* in March 2011, the leading star of the English women's game, Maggie Alphonsi, identified a change in attitudes following the most recent World Cup. She noticed then for the first time when people approached her after a game they would say that it had been a really great game or that she was a really good rugby player. 'The "woman" bit they used to put in seems to have gone now... It's not women's rugby. It's just rugby.'

## THE SECRET RUGBY SISTERHOOD

The early history of women's rugby seems to be shrouded in mystery, as early female players of the game kept their sporting exploits hidden. An attempt to organise a women's tour of New Zealand in 1891 was cancelled after a public outcry. There are stories of women's games being played behind closed doors in France and England in the early 1900s, with women wearing bathing hats to prevent their hair being caught up as they were tackled. Women's charity games were arranged during the First World War and in 1917 Cardiff Ladies beat Newport Ladies 6–0 at Cardiff Arms Park. But in 1920 a rugby league game in Australia between two women's sides caused a clampdown from the game's authorities.

In the swinging sixties attitudes began to change and students in Edinburgh formed the first recorded university women's side in 1962. The WRFU was formed in England in 1983 and gradually the women's game has grown from there.

The first international women's tournament, called Rugbyfest, was held in Christchurch, New Zealand in 1990. This saw a New Zealand women's team beating a combined World XV as the finale after a round-robin tournament between a handful of national and club sides. The following year the first women's Rugby World Cup was staged in Wales, although the International Rugby Board snootily withheld its approval. The USA became the first women's rugby world champions after beating England in the final.

As the 1994 women's World Cup was planned for the Netherlands, palpitating administrators in the IRB threatened sanctions against any participating nations. As a result the Dutch withdrew their offer to host the tournament and the event was hastily shifted to Scotland, who were presumably a little less bothered about the officials and their ungallant disapproval. England won, defeating the USA in the final.

Two years later the IRB established a Women's Advisory Committee, as rugby administrators do love a committee. It seems that as long as there are some chaps in blazers sat around a table, someone to take minutes, apologies for absence being noted, and space on the agenda for 'any other business', then things like sanctioning and supporting a women's version of the World Cup is possible. The tournament with official approval eventually took place in the Netherlands in 1998 and has continued every four years since.

In 2014 12 sides assembled in France for the biggest women's World Cup tournament yet. After a group stage involving three groups of four teams, a rather ingenious and inclusive format allowed play-offs for all 12 placings. Large French crowds demonstrated how far the game has progressed, and during the group stage there was a peak TV audience of two million. Some 20,000 supporters filled the Stade Jean-Bouin, home of the Parisian side Stade Français, to watch a double-header made up of the third place play-off between Ireland and France and then the final between Canada and England. France comfortably secured third place and the English defeated Canada by 21 points to 9. The victorious English team was made up of plumbers, vets, teachers, police officers and students. The majority had to take three months' unpaid leave in order to play in the tournament. On the back of the women's success the English RFU announced that it would extend professional contracts to 20 players, allowing them to train full time and inspire the next generation of girls to play rugby.

# GREAT FEMALE PLAYERS

## KATY McLEAN

When the BBC Sports Personality Award for Team of the Year was presented to the England Women's Rugby Union team in 2014, following their victory in the World Cup final against Canada, England captain Katy McLean was presented with the coveted trophy. McLean's career was far from straightforward and sums up how much women's rugby has changed in England in just a few short years.

Born in South Shields in 1985, Katy was introduced to rugby by watching her dad play at her local club in Westoe. From standing on the touchline in her wellies, it wasn't long before she was on the pitch in a pair of rugby boots, playing in a mixed team up until the age of 12. Even though Katy was the only girl, she was a feisty scrum half and always in the thick of the action.

But from the age of 13, insurance and health and safety reasons meant that rugby-mad girls like Katy couldn't play in mixed teams, and with no girls' rugby network to speak of, Katy drifted away from the game and into hockey, netball, football and cross-country running. Fortunately, when she was 16 she entered a regional tag-rugby tournament and was spotted by a North East under-16s team. That led to trials for the England squad. Ten years later she was lifting the World Cup trophy.

McLean combined a rugby career with teaching. After a day with her reception class in Sunderland she would either train with her local club in Darlington, head for the gym or meet up with the England coach, Gary Street, to work on her fly-half game. Often the two would spend hours kicking the ball to each other on a dark and cold playing field somewhere in North Yorkshire.

As already mentioned, the RFU celebrated the women's World Cup victory by awarding 20 England players full-time contracts, which allowed Katy and her teammates to give up their day jobs and concentrate on representing their country and playing the game they all loved. No wonder the squad all looked so happy, in their matching blue evening gowns, as they stood alongside Katy as she accepted the BBC trophy on their behalf and gracefully thanked all the people who had transformed women's rugby in England for good.

## ELLIA GREEN

In the early 1990s Australian TV motoring presenter Evan Green and his wife adopted two young siblings, a boy and a girl, both born in Fiji. The girl, only two days old, they named Ellia. Sadly, Evan died only a couple of years later, leaving his wife Yolanta to raise the children alone. Ellia joined an athletics club at the age of six and went on to represent Australia in the 100 and 200 metres and the long jump at the World Junior Championships. Her cousins convinced her to try rugby and, with her natural speed from the athletics track, she rapidly found herself in the Australian women's rugby sevens side. She didn't really understand the new game but her mother said to her, 'You know what, Ellia, when you get that ball don't let anyone touch you, you just run.' And that's what she did.

Her mother, who was diagnosed twice with breast cancer, is a huge source of inspiration for the Australian winger. Ellia writes 'Mum' on her wrist strapping before every game to remind her of what her family has been through. Known as the Green Machine, Ellia scored a brilliant 80-metre try in an exhibition match against Canada and secured a place in the team travelling to Rio for the return of rugby to the Olympics in 2016, although her mother had confidently already booked the plane tickets. Bursting with pride, Yolanta witnessed her daughter come off the bench in the Olympic final to score the try that effectively sealed the victory for the Pearls against the Black Ferns of New Zealand. Speaking after the game, Ellia said, 'We've just made Australian history, rugby history.' And she was right.

## HEATHER FISHER

Getting naked after rugby games has been an all too common feature of the men's game for many years. So it should have been no surprise when the England women went one better and got naked before a tournament, though of course they did it in a slightly more sophisticated and intelligent manner than the boys might have done. Five members of the Great Britain women's rugby team appeared in the naked edition of *Women's Health* magazine in 2016 prior to setting off for the Olympics in Rio. They did it to highlight body confidence issues by showing dramatically how their different body shapes help them to succeed as a team. For one team member the photo shoot was particularly poignant.

Heather Fisher's road to the Olympics had been difficult. She had difficulties with food as a young woman, when her parents were going through a difficult divorce and she used food as a way to get back some sort of control over her life. A coach took her to one side and said that she would never become an athlete if she didn't eat and from that point she began to adopt healthier eating habits.

She battled with body confidence when she made the change from bobsleigh to rugby. The transition from pushing a sledge for one explosive burst at the start of a run to pushing in scrums, rucks and mauls for much of an 80-minute game meant that her shoulders shrank and her legs got much bigger. But she got over it, deciding that she wasn't training to look good but simply to be more effective at her new chosen sport.

Then, around the time of the 2010 World Cup, she started suffering with alopecia, partially, she thought, as a result of the stress of the tournament. England's women narrowly missed out on victory, losing to New Zealand in the final, and Heather lost most of her hair in huge clumps. But four years later, in 2014, she was in England's World Cup-winning squad and, although injury kept her out of the final against Canada, after the tournament she secured one of the full-time contracts granted to the England team. Nothing now was going to stop her from getting to the Olympics in Rio, and with her strength and aggression she played a key role in helping Team GB women's sevens side into the semi-finals, where they narrowly missed out on a medal. With a shaved head and powerful frame, Heather Fisher stands out on the pitch and demonstrates that rugby is a sport that not only welcomes different body types but one that positively celebrates them.

## ISADORA CERULLO

Isadora Cerullo was born in North Carolina to Brazilian parents who had fled to the USA to escape their home country's military dictatorship. Their daughter played soccer and competed in cross-country running at high school, but joined the rugby club when she went off to study medicine at Columbia University. Meanwhile, back in Brazil, Olympic coaches were looking across the world for athletes with a Brazilian connection to bolster their teams for the 2016 games. As the host nation, Brazil had automatically qualified for competitions that it might not normally enter and so was prepared to offer try-outs to players with a parent or grandparent born in the country. Cerullo put her medical career on hold and headed for Brazil and a once-in-a-lifetime opportunity. Her girlfriend, Marjorie Enya, travelled with her and the pair set up home in São Paulo as Cerullo focused on making it into the Brazilian squad. Cerullo not only did that, but within a year had won a bronze medal at the 2015 Pan American games. Enya started to make plans of her own and lined up a role for herself as a volunteer manager at the Deodoro Stadium where the Olympic rugby sevens tournament was to be held.

After Brazil's final game in the tournament, the ninth-place play-off against Japan, Enya grabbed a stadium microphone and in front of the world's TV cameras made an emotional speech and proposed to Cerullo. Much to the delight of the crowd and her fellow teammates, Cerullo accepted and the TV images were seen all around the world. Speaking afterwards, Enya told BBC Sport, 'I know rugby people are amazing and that they would embrace it. I wanted to show people that love wins.'

# PICK A POSITION

· · · · · · · · · · · · · · · · · · · · · · · · · · · · · · · · · · · · · · · · · · · ·

> *❝ The appeal of rugby for the player*
> *is that it is designed to cater for men*
> *of any physique as long as they have that*
> *vital fire which is worth a ton of theory. ❞*
> **BOB STUART, NEW ZEALAND RUGBY PLAYER**

One of the many reasons why rugby is such a great team game is that it celebrates and capitalises on our differences, finding the perfect role for everyone. We come in a wide range of bizarre shapes and sizes, but for every single one there is a perfect position on the rugby pitch. Different personalities may thrive in different places, too. Every role in a rugby team has its own particular pleasures, as the following list is designed to illustrate.

# RUGBY UNION

LOOSE-HEAD PROP

HOOKER

TIGHT-HEAD PROP

SECOND ROW

SECOND ROW

BLIND-SIDE FLANKER

OPEN-SIDE FLANKER

NUMBER 8

SCRUM HALF

FLY HALF

INSIDE CENTRE

OUTSIDE CENTRE

LEFT WING

RIGHT WING

FULL BACK

## PROP

Props are the two players on either side of the front row of a scrum. The joy of this position is in the pure battle of physical strength and technique with the opposite number. Props are also allowed to eat a few more of the pies and are excused from running-around duties, as a little extra body weight is important in those front-row battles.

## HOOKER

Hookers play in the middle of the front row of the scrum and have the pleasure of pretty much guaranteed contact with the ball, as it is their job to hook it back from the middle of the scrum. Hookers are also given the task of throwing the ball in at the lineout and can, over the years, gradually earn respect from their teammates for simply being able to throw the ball in a reasonably straight line at a convenient height for a pre-arranged member of their team to catch.

## LOCK

Players in this position can bask in the glory of being the 'powerhouse' of the scrum. A lock's job is to push the props forward in the scrum with their shoulders and lock out their legs and prevent the props from being pushed backwards. Partially because of where the locks are expected to put their heads, squashed between the backsides of the hooker and the props, they will also be more likely than many other players to acquire the ultimate rugby status symbol, a cauliflower ear.

## CAULIFLOWER EAR

Cauliflower ear, or *hematoma auris*, is caused when the ear is hit and a blood clot collects between the cartilage and the other layers around it. The cartilage then dies and forms fibrous tissue and the outer ear becomes permanently deformed. Psychiatrists in the 1800s thought it was linked to insanity, but some rugby players refuse to have it treated, regarding it as a badge of honour.

## FLANKER

The great thing about this position is that flankers are able to get out of the scrum first, avoiding any unpleasant pile-ups, as they only really need to hang loosely to one side or the other. As a result flankers will also often be the first forward to get to the ball or to get to an opponent with the ball – so if you enjoy running with the ball or tackling anyone else with it, this is almost definitely the place to be.

## NUMBER 8

This is the position right at the back of the scrum usually reserved for the most experienced and capable of all the forwards. The number 8 is the only player who is allowed to break off from the scrum and pick up the ball and run with it. Alternatively they can choose to allow the backs to have the ball if they prefer. Number 8 is pretty much in charge and everyone knows it.

## SCRUM HALF

The joy of being a scrum half is getting to boss all the forwards around in spite of being approximately half their size. The scrum half's job is to lurk behind the forwards, trying to keep out of trouble and extracting the ball once in a while to give to the backs. A scrum half needs to be brave, fearless and able to pass quickly and accurately to the...

## FLY HALF (OR A BIT STAND-OFFISH)

One of the glamorous positions, the fly half is able to enjoy the game without worrying too much about whether it might mess up their hair. The backs might not get the ball too often from the forwards, especially on a wet muddy pitch, but when they do, it is up to the fly half to decide what to do with it. They can kick for distance and get the team out of trouble in defence, or set up a clever running move with the rest of the backs. The fly half calls the moves and is the envy of all the other backs.

## CENTRE

There is much fun to be had here either tackling or shimmying and sidestepping with the ball through the opposition's attempts at tackles, setting up and occasionally even scoring tries. Typically centres will be some of the finer physical specimens among the backs and most of their game happens in the open periods of play. A centre's efforts will be seen and appreciated by any spectators who happen to be around.

There are two centres, an inside centre and an outside centre, but that doesn't mean that one of them conducts the entire game from within the clubhouse. The inside centre is the one

FOR THE LOVE OF RUGBY

closest to the fly half, probably the more senior of the two and the one most likely to be flattened when an attacking move goes wrong.

## WINGER

The wing is a great place for a player carrying less weight who can therefore run a little quicker than their teammates. On the wing they can keep well out of trouble for much of the game and, very occasionally, when it has been through everyone else, will find themselves with the ball in their hands and a very short distance to run and score a try.

## FULL BACK

Before retiring from the game everyone should play here at least once. This position is the last line of defence and, although that can be a little nerve-racking, the full back is a total hero if they make a try-saving tackle. They will also be under a lot of high kicks and, if they can catch the ball without dropping it, will have the opportunity to have a nice long run with it before anyone can attempt to stop them.

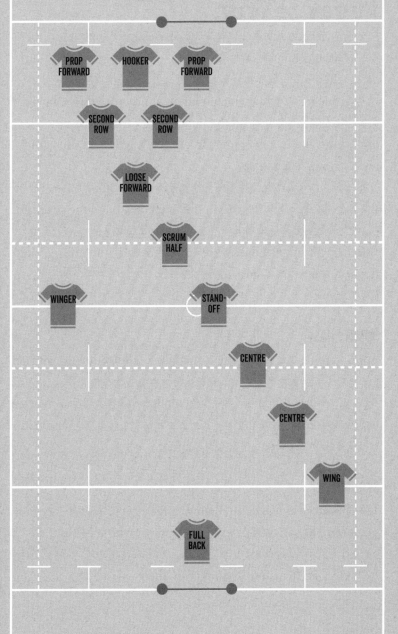

# RUGBY LEAGUE

# RUGBY LEAGUE

In rugby league there are only 13 players on the pitch, so there is a little more multitasking and the players tend to be a little more alike and interchangeable. Rugby league teams seem to have come to an arrangement that means there is rarely any real pushing in the scrums, so the bulk of the forwards is much less important. Instead, everyone in a rugby league side needs to be lean, strong, fit and fast.

The positions are much the same as in rugby union but without the two flankers. Forwards are still expected to be the strongest players, able to break through tackles and make important hard yards up the pitch. Backs are expected to be a little quicker, more nimble and able to make the final breakthrough to score tries.

## DUMMY HALF

After a tackle, the person being tackled is allowed to get up and heel the ball back to a teammate to continue the play. The player who picks up the ball is called the dummy half and anyone can have a go. It is typically the hooker's job but if they are being tackled then someone else will step in.

## SCRUM HALF

This position in league is actually a little more like the fly half in union. The scrum half will be the player who receives the ball passed from behind each tackle and will determine, with the fly half, the way the game unfolds from there.

## OLD RUGBY PLAYERS NEVER DIE – THEY JUST CHANGE POSITIONS

Very few of us stay exactly the same shape and retain the same levels of physical fitness throughout our lives. Rugby turns out to be a remarkably accommodating sport and, as your body changes over time, so can your position. Many a young winger has, with the passage of years, acquired a few more muscles and perhaps a little more weight around the middle and found themselves in the front row at a later stage in their career. England hooker Tom Youngs started his rugby as a centre before a coach at Leicester Tigers gently encouraged him to sample the delights to be found in the middle of the scrum. Many an amateur end-of-season tour fixture has involved players trying their hand at a new position just for fun and an additional challenge, to see the game from a new perspective.

# TRAINING

························································

*❝ Throughout the week I have one side of me that does all the preparation and resting and eating well and training, then it hands all that over to the second individual, and that other individual is a hugely competitive, instinctive one who is just desperate to win. He is a bit of a monster, actually. ❞*
**JONNY WILKINSON, ENGLAND RUGBY PLAYER**

For the casual player, training in rugby is by no means compulsory. For those aiming for a place in the first team, it might be a good idea to turn up and train once in a while to impress the selectors and remind them that you exist. However, there are plenty of second-, third- and fourth-team captains who will happily give you a game, regardless of whether you have made it to the midweek fitness and drills session.

But building your strength, confidence and ball-handling skills will always be useful come the weekend games. Training sessions are also a good opportunity to learn from senior players some of the tricks, techniques and set-piece moves that will make your 80 minutes of competitive rugby on Saturday afternoons all the more enjoyable.

More importantly, training regularly with a rugby club is one of the best ways to improve your level of fitness and general well-being. For many people, training in a group is much more motivational than training on your own. There will probably be someone else close to your size and general fitness and skill level to work alongside.

Most community-based clubs will warmly welcome you at training on one or two evenings a week. Under floodlights for much of the year, amateur coaches will run prospective players through a series of warm-ups, stretches, fitness routines, drills and exercises to get you into the best possible shape to represent the club well.

## THE CLASSIC TRAINING GRID

One of the most popular and common training drills is when the players line up on four corners of a square, approximately 5 metres apart. Players will then, one at a time, run with a ball diagonally into the middle of the square and then pass the ball to a player coming from the opposite corner.

Players have to keep their wits about them to dodge players running and passing at 90 degrees to their line while making sure that they catch the pass that is coming to them and deliver a sympathetic and easy-to-catch pass to the next person. Once the players have mastered this at a jogging pace, coaches will speed things up a bit or add new complications.

Players must concentrate on getting their hands ready in a position to accept a pass and communicate verbally and non-verbally with teammates in order to avoid the embarrassment of dropping a ball. After five or ten minutes, making short accurate passes becomes second nature.

## TRAINING KIT

One thing to remember in training is that no one wants to get themselves injured unnecessarily. For that reason, a lot of club training sessions will involve large quantities of foam, in various shapes and sizes, wrapped up in brightly coloured waterproof vinyl. Tackle pads are used to allow players to train hard in simulated contact situations while reducing the knocks and injuries that might otherwise occur.

## TOUCH RUGBY

Another great way of avoiding injuries at training is to play touch rugby. This is essentially the same as full-contact rugby except that a tackle is deemed to have been made when one player touches an opponent, ideally with two hands, on the hips below the waistband. The tackled player then stops and heels the ball back to another teammate for play to continue.

As it takes the contact, rucks and mauls out of the game, touch rugby is a great way for players of all levels of ability within a team to get the ball in their hands and practise running at gaps, timing their moves, catching, passing and generally communicating better with other players.

Touch rugby has the added advantage that it can also be played all year round and in mixed teams, so the men's and the women's sides in a club can occasionally train together.

Some clubs use it as a gentle introduction to the sport for new players before persuading them to try the full-contact version.

## LINEOUT MOVES

Training sessions are the perfect places to compose the complex series of code words and choreographed switches of position, dummy jumps and lifts that make up the modern lineout. When your side is awarded a lineout throw-in, every effort must be made to ensure that one of your own side catches the ball cleanly. The advantage lies in your teammates knowing where the ball is going to go and precisely when it is going to be thrown, and having a 'jumper' in the air at the right time in the right place.

Hours can be spent at the training pitch establishing new codes, signals and ways to trick the opposition and hide your own side's intentions. At the very least, though, a basic code is required to signal whether the ball is going to be aimed at the front, middle or back of the lineout.

Hookers also need to put in a good few hours on the training pitch to be able to throw the oval ball in a perfectly straight line to a predictable height and length. Standing on the try line and aiming the ball at a fixed point on the goalposts will help the aspiring hooker to get their eye in. Varying the throwing distance from the goalposts at 5 metres, 7 metres and 9 metres will simulate the conditions for a throw to the front, middle and back of the line.

## SCRUM MACHINES

In the late 1970s Tim Francis, a teacher at Dulwich College in south London, had a little sideline making and selling exercise mats. His school had always had a strong rugby side and Francis began thinking about building a training machine that would allow the forwards to safely train for the increasingly technical aspects of scrummaging.

In the staff common room, he started to build experimental models out of cotton reels and matchsticks, before moving on to full-scale prototypes made from 200-litre drums and planks of wood. By 1980 he had given up the day job, moved to Devon and was working full time to create the Powerhouse, the first mass-produced and marketed scrum machine.

The first outing for the Powerhouse was at a Rosslyn Park National Schools Sevens tournament in March 1982. The machine was left at the side of the pitches for teams to try out in between games. By the end of the day Francis had orders for six machines and the business was up and running.

England prop Jeff Probyn, recalling an early scrum machine he used at Bath University that used hydraulic pressure to simulate the forces an opposition pack might apply, said, 'The first time they released the pressure I was literally pushed through the back of my boots because the pressure split the seams.'

Today scrum machines have become much more sophisticated, with sensors and computers to calculate the combined forces being applied. As the laws about the scrum seem to change almost every season, the latest scrum machines even have alarms set to predict when the referee might blow up for an infringement.

# GILBERT – A RUGBY BRAND WITH AN IMPRESSIVE HERITAGE

William Gilbert owned a shoe- and boot-making business located close to Rugby School. He turned his hand to making rugby balls for the boys using an inflated pig's bladder encased in four leather panels; the oval shape of the ball came from the shape of the pig's bladder. Making the balls was not a particularly pleasant task: the bladders had to be blown up in their fresh, smelly, 'green' state, using lung power and a clay pipe. Gilbert's nephew James gained a reputation among the pupils at Rugby School as being 'a wonder of lung strength and blew even the big match balls up tight'.

Their effort clearly paid off. Gilbert's early rugby balls were displayed and won medals at the Great Exhibition in 1851 and the Great London Exposition of 1862. The ball changed shape over the years as the game evolved, becoming smaller and more pointed. In 1890 the first laws were introduced governing the size and shape of the ball and today the Gilbert brand name adorns the official match ball of the Rugby World Cup.

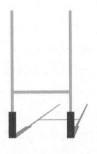

# THE DIET OF CHAMPIONS

Nutrition is increasingly important for rugby players who want to get their bodies into the optimum physical condition for a game. A good diet provides the raw materials to build and repair muscles, as well as providing the energy to last the intense 80 minutes of a game. Top-level players will have a strictly controlled diet, personally tailored to their own body and playing position, but even the lowest-level amateur player can benefit from the professional rugby players' dietary tips.

## FLUIDS

Getting enough liquid on board, in a form other than beer, is hugely important for rugby players. Top international players have been known to lose up to 3.5 kg in weight during a game, and that is almost entirely down to water loss. A lack of fluids leads to an immediate drop in performance. Advice given to the England squad in 2002 was that players should drink at least 3 litres a day and that a 3 per cent reduction in hydration would lead to a 10 per cent reduction in strength and an 8 per cent reduction in speed.

## CARBOHYDRATES

Carbohydrates provide energy for training and playing, and are absolutely essential for rugby players. Complex carbs are best because they release their energy slowly and steadily throughout the day; soybeans, sweet potatoes, lentils, apples, oranges, wholewheat pasta, brown rice, wholewheat bread, oats and fresh vegetables are good three hours before a game. Sugary refined carbs can be good after a game once you have properly rehydrated, to get energy quickly back into the muscles.

It is important to match the calories going in with the energy that you expend. For the average British male, who now weighs around 83 kg (13 stone), 80 minutes of rugby burns off 1,089 calories. That is the equivalent of six pints of beer. Perfect for the post-match celebration in the clubhouse. In fact many clubs will happily sell you the beer in a 6-pint jug for your ease and convenience.

## PROTEIN

Protein is important for muscle repair and regrowth, and professional players will be advised to think about including protein with every meal. Eggs, lean meat, poultry and fish are all good. You should avoid processed meats such as pâté, salami and sausages, and anything that is deep-fried in batter. It is important to keep taking on protein even on rest days, as that is when the body builds new muscle.

## FAT

The good news for rugby players is that not all fat is bad for you. You should of course avoid saturated fats (butter and lard) and trans fats, which are formed when fats are fried, meaning burgers and fried food are pretty much out. Cold-water fish like salmon, trout, mackerel and sardines are packed full of oils that are so good for you they have been declared to be utterly 'essential'. Olive oil is also tremendously good for you, so much so that perhaps the traditional rugby song should be rewritten...

" *Four and twenty bottles of extra virgin olive oil went down to Inverness...* "

# THE PROFESSIONALS

································································

*It takes two hours to get ready – hot bath, shave my legs and face, moisturise, put fake tan on and do my hair – which takes a bit of time.*

**GAVIN HENSON, WELSH RUGBY PLAYER**

The story of how rugby union turned professional is intrinsically linked to the split with rugby league and the complex and difficult relationship between the two separate codes of the game.

In the early 1900s, clubs in the south-west of England attempted to form a western branch of the northern union that had split from the RFU over the issue of paying players. Numerous clubs and players were banned, including one James Peters, who had been the first black man to play rugby union for England.

Peters had played for England against Scotland and France and had thoroughly irritated a touring side from apartheid South Africa when he appeared in the line-up for a Devon RFC side that the South Africans were due to play. The South African High Commissioner had to persuade his fellow countrymen to take to the field as he feared a riot from the impatient crowd. Shamefully, Peters was, however, left out of the England squad that played South Africa later in the tour, purely on racial grounds. Indeed, he was not to play another game for England and was later suspended for accepting payment from Devon Rugby Club. He headed north and saw out his career playing in rugby league for Barrow-in-Furness and then St Helens before retiring from the game altogether in 1914.

For many years rugby union struggled to hold on to its amateur status. At the top level players were expected to make a substantial commitment to keeping fit, training and playing, and those senior players could see fellow sportsmen and women earning a respectable living in other games.

Some have argued that turning a blind eye to some of the payments to Welsh players prevented the growth of rugby league on the other side of Offa's Dyke. When the Welsh international Arthur Gould was awarded the deeds to his house in 1897, the RFU declared him a professional and banned all clubs and players from playing with him. Only when the Welsh Rugby Union withdrew from the international board and began making moves to join the NRFU was a 'compromise' reached and those blind eyes were turned.

## BEATING THE SYSTEM

As rugby union grew in popularity during the 1980s and more money found its way into the sport, players found a range of ways to get around the rules and make a living doing what they loved:

1.  Being given a not-too-arduous 'job' by a generous club benefactor with a big business that allowed extensive periods of absence for training and fixtures.

2.  Being employed by the club as a 'coach' or 'groundsman' with no real duties other than training.

3.  Being paid for personal appearances by corporate entertainment types.

4.  Being paid for endorsing products.

5.  Being given boot money – whereby players would find some cash rolled up in their boots in the changing rooms.

6.  Giving in and finally going off to play rugby league.

Aussie rugby legend David Campese summed it up when he declared:

> ❝ *I'm still an amateur, of course, but I became rugby's first millionaire five years ago.* ❞

# 57 OLD FARTS

Players and regulators were often at loggerheads over their interpretation of laws that stated what they could and could not be paid for. Matters came to a head in 1995, when in a TV interview in the build-up to the World Cup that year, England captain Will Carling publicly and memorably attacked the people who were in charge of the game, saying,

> **"** *If the game is run properly as a professional game, you do not need 57 old farts running rugby.* **"**

The old-fart-in-chief at the time was RFU secretary Dudley Wood, who had adjudicated disputes over payments for personal appearances and product endorsements, including one case of £100 in Burton clothing vouchers, which were awarded to Simon Hodgkinson for winning a Player of Merit contest.

The old farts were the 57 members of the council of the RFU who govern the game, drawn from the constituent bodies that make up the rugby union, including representatives from each county, along with the Army, Royal Navy and Royal Air Force's rugby sides. After a good deal of harrumphing, the decision was made to allow players to be paid to play and the character of the game at a senior level changed forever.

## OR DID IT?

The spirit of amateurism still lives on in the vast majority of clubs around the world. In England the old farts are still in charge, although now there are around 60 of them. A few were added to represent players and referees, and there is one to represent women and girls.

In 2011 a lengthy report was commissioned from the leading international law firm Slaughter and May, which concluded that the way rugby was administered could perhaps be a little more efficient. The old farts fought back and, after an 18-month consultation period, the sport's rulers concluded that the sport should stay more or less as it is.

For all the frustrations and limitations of its old-fashioned nature, there is something quite heart-warming about the way rugby is run in England. In spite of the sport being a huge business, with TV revenues swelling the coffers of the leading clubs, it remains a game that is effectively owned and democratically controlled by elected representatives of all the clubs, down to those in the very lowest leagues or those merely playing occasional games against casual sides. Anyone with a real love of the game and enough time on their hands could one day find themselves being a club chairperson. Once you have done that, it is only a short jump onto a county committee and, before you know it, you too could become an old fart on the RFU council and have a say in the way rugby develops and changes in the future.

## THOSE OLD FARTS IN FULL

All sections of the game are represented on the RFU council these days:

- 35 representing the constituent bodies (28 counties, with the larger ones having more than one representative)
- 7 representing schools
- 4 presidential roles
- 3 armed forces
- 2 International Rugby Board

- 2 national

- 1 co-opted

- 1 representing referees

- 1 representing players

- 1 specifically representing female players

- 1 chairperson

- 1 chief executive

# THE CROSS-CODE CHALLENGE

Fortunately, the two codes have now pretty much buried the hatchet and permit players to transfer between rugby league and rugby union. Some great players, such as Jonathan Davies and Jason Robinson, have now played both codes, and both versions of the game have almost certainly benefited as a result. Converts from league are now regularly welcomed into the union fold. Andy Farrell made the switch from league in 2005 and now coaches the England backs, including his son, the fly half Owen Farrell. The switch, however, is not always successful. Sam Burgess moved from league to union and controversially found his way into the England squad just in time for the 2015 World Cup. When England, who were the hosts of the competition, were knocked out in the group stage, many blamed the decision to play the inexperienced former league player in the centres. Burgess returned to rugby league, travelling Down Under and signing for the South Sydney Rabbitohs.

As relations thawed between rugby union and league, a clash of the codes was organised in 1996 between Bath RFC, that season's winners of the Pilkington Cup and the Courage League, and Wigan, the previous season's RFL Championship title-holders. Over two legs the sides played a full game of rugby league at Old Trafford in Manchester and then a full game of rugby union at Twickenham. With two tries from Martin 'Chariots' Offiah and more from Jason Robinson, Scott Quinnell and others, Wigan finished the first leg comfortably ahead at 82–6.

Two and a half weeks later, the sides met at Twickenham for the rugby union leg. In the first half Wigan struggled in the eight-man scrum and conceded a penalty try for collapsing repeatedly. Bath, with international players Mike Catt and Phil de Glanville, were well ahead at half time but in the second half the sides were much more evenly matched. As Bath began to tire, the fitter Wigan players matched them point for point. They scored two phenomenal tries which both started from behind their own try line, Jason Robinson demonstrating the blistering pace that had earned him the nickname Billy Whizz. The game ended with Bath the winners, but by a closer margin of 44–17.

Jason Robinson would subsequently transfer from league to union and would win 51 union caps for England to add to his collection of 12 league caps for Great Britain and seven for England. Scott Quinnell, who had switched codes two years earlier after leaving Llanelli RFC to join Wigan, switched back to union in 1996 when he joined Richmond, and went on to play in the Welsh side that reached the World Cup quarter-finals in 1999.

# WHEN THE CAP DOESN'T FIT

When rugby union turned professional in 1995 it caused a major upheaval in the game, especially in England. Until that point the major clubs competed in the Courage League, but it was a fairly relaxed affair with the fixtures being organised on an ad-hoc basis between the clubs themselves. Professional sport meant a more professionally run Premiership with fixtures rather more fixed to suit television schedules. Revenues were pooled and arrangements made for a salary cap and a fixed maximum total wage bill for all clubs to allay the fears that an unbridled free market would unbalance the teams and destroy the competition.

The French, meanwhile, had an established senior-level club competition that had been around more or less since 1892. Players in the French Top 14 league also enjoyed a significantly higher salary cap than their English equivalents. The English rugby authorities attempted to stem the flow of top stars heading over the Channel in search of higher wages by insisting that only those playing in domestic clubs would be eligible for selection to the national side. That hasn't stopped the likes of Jonny Wilkinson and others heading to the south of France after their international career has come to a natural end.

The top French clubs have stolen a march on the rest of the Northern Hemisphere in terms of investment, attendances and budgets. In the 2009–10 season the leading French club, Toulouse, enjoyed a €33 million budget, whereas Leicester, the wealthiest English club that season, could only rustle up €21 million. French clubs were allowed by the French National Rugby League to spend around €10 million on the players' wage bill, whereas the figure in England was roughly half that amount.

## FILLING THE STANDS

Attendance at top-level club rugby has increased, however, since the professional era began. The average crowd at a Premiership game in 1997–98 was around 6,000, but by 2014–15 this had increased to 13,611. Many clubs will also hold one or two special games a season where they slash the prices to attract a bigger crowd and move their games to Twickenham or Wembley to accommodate them all.

As the international game has become more popular over recent decades, the opportunity to see the global stars playing throughout the season in club fixtures has no doubt helped to swell the crowds and the coffers of the top sides. A study by sports economists at University College Dublin, however, found that the main factor that affects attendance levels is simply how often the team wins at home. Regular home wins set the turnstiles spinning, so the financial rewards for the stronger home sides are significant and growing.

Even players in the lower leagues will occasionally benefit from the arrival of professionalism. Every so often a local side will find itself a wealthy benefactor prepared to pay players a token amount per game in an attempt to build a stronger club. Although many argue that the payments distort local leagues and divert money from investment in new facilities, for many young men the cash can be a very welcome source of additional income and an incentive to train and play well.

# TYPICAL WEEK OF A PREMIERSHIP RUGBY PLAYER

## Monday

- Swimming pool recovery session
- Medical screening for any injuries picked up at the weekend
- Match video analysis
- Light run-out – touch rugby

## Tuesday

- Contact rugby session – 75 per cent intensity
- Backs' moves and kicking practice
- Set-piece training – lineouts and scrums
- Weight training

## Wednesday

Day off

## Thursday

- Contact rugby session – 75 per cent intensity
- Backs' moves and kicking practice
- Set-piece training – lineouts and scrums
- Weight training

## Friday

Team run – jogging through the planned plays with the team selected for the game

## Saturday

- Light breakfast
- Walk through the moves for the day with the squad
- Primer session – stretches
- Light lunch three hours before kick-off
- Pre-match warm up
- Final motivational team talks
- The game
- Ice bath

## Sunday

Day off

# POWER PACKS

Tom Fordyce of BBC Sport has calculated the average weight and height of an England international forward over the past five decades:

| YEAR | WEIGHT | HEIGHT |
|---|---|---|
| 1962 | 92.5 kg | 1.83 m |
| 1972 | 97.75 kg | 1.89 m |
| 1982 | 89.9 kg | 1.86 m |
| 1992 | 106.5 kg | 1.88 m |
| 2002 | 110.1 kg | 1.86 m |
| 2012 | 112.9 kg | 1.92 m |

# THE MANAGEMENT TEAM

The back-room support behind a successful team can make the difference between winning and losing. As described in his book *Winning!*, head coach Clive Woodward assembled the following group that took the England national team to World Cup victory in 2003:

- Team manager
- Coach
- Assistant coach
- Assistant coach (kicking)
- Team doctor
- Team physiotherapist

- Team fitness advisor

- Scrummaging advisor

- Team masseur

- Video analyst

- Press officer

- Baggage master

- Referee advisor

- Head of performance services

- PA

- Media relations manager

# THE CLUBHOUSE

• • • • • • • • • • • • • • • • • • • • • • • • • • • • • • • • • • • •

*❝ The spirit was excellent. Yes, we were all naked together at times, but so what? The only chaps who were perhaps a bit shy initially were those with small willies. ❞*

**SOUTH AFRICAN RUGBY PLAYER ON THE COUNTRY'S 2003 WORLD CUP SQUAD**

Probably more than any other sport, rugby has developed an image that is just as much about how players socialise and celebrate as it is about how they play the game. Very few people would confidently predict the likely goings-on at a cycling or athletic club social gathering. Rugby clubs, on the other hand, have a bit of a reputation.

From the moment the referee blows the final whistle to when the bar manager calls last orders, rugby clubs still provide one of the most spirited, hearty and hospitable environments for players and spectators to recover, rehydrate and unwind after a game.

Ah yes, the bar. The place for a quiet pint followed, as former English international Gareth Chilcott once said, by 15 noisy ones. The songs and the antics that come after a game are tame compared with what might have just happened on the pitch, but they are all part of the joyful rugby experience. Keeping brewers in business while setting innuendo and double entendre to music, the rugby club bar can be a boisterous but utterly brilliant institution.

Sociologists and political theorists do rather fret about the decline in the numbers of people who are members of clubs and societies (something they call 'social capital'). Meanwhile, around the world and in the nation that gave birth to the game, rugby clubs continue to survive in good numbers and host some of the most spirited post-match celebrations and other social events imaginable.

# THE RISE AND RISE OF RUGBY CLUBS

Across the history of the game there have been a few particular periods when rugby clubs have grown significantly in strength and number:

- In the 1870s when the RFU was formed, the new association gave clubs an impetus to become constituted and acquire a clubhouse.

- In the 1920s club numbers increased again as rugby became seen as a mark of middle-class respectability. The 'better' schools switched from the association game to rugby and their old boys formed new clubs when they left.

- In the 1950s, improving economic conditions meant that rugby clubs had to compete with alternative leisure pursuits, and televised international fixtures led to fewer people watching local games from the touchlines. Clubs needed to improve and improvise to survive as their revenues declined. In Wales, Llanharan RFC built changing rooms from surplus RAF units and some clubs pooled their clothing ration coupons in order to get enough kit to play in.

■ In the swinging sixties, numbers surged again as rugby union became a little more democratic and spread further across society. Michael Green, author of the brilliant book *The Art of Coarse Rugby*, argues that rugby 'began to be discussed in workshops as well as boardrooms... and few clubs bother about where a player went to school'.

# ACADEMIC SEAL OF APPROVAL FOR POST-MATCH CELEBRATIONS

Today rugby still wins when it comes to socialising. A learned academic report entitled 'Social and Economic Value of Sport in Ireland' by Tony Fahey and Liam Delaney of Ireland's Economic and Social Research Institute found that rugby generates the greatest frequency of socialising among players. Eighty-six per cent of Irish rugby players socialise with other rugby players at least once a week, and certainly more often than they socialise with university academics.

Rugby is a sociable game and, as it turns out, is good for your soul as well as keeping you fit. The same report found that 'members of sports clubs report higher levels of physical and mental well-being throughout the life cycle than the rest of the population'. They concluded that sports club membership is part of a package that helps people live a healthier life and grow old more successfully than the rest of the population.

In 2003, rugby union became Britain's second-most-popular sport after football, according to a national opinion poll, when 27 per cent of British adults expressed an interest in the sport. This might have had something to do with the success of the England team in winning the Rugby World Cup that year, but it meant that more than 15 million adults were now interested in rugby union. Rugby league came in eleventh in the same poll, while union's popularity had also spread beyond its traditionally white, male, middle-class audience, with interest increasing among women, the young and even a few people who had been educated in a comprehensive school.

## BEER, BEER AND MORE BEER

Where there are rugby players, there will be beer, and the success of rugby clubs has often been linked to healthy profits behind the bar. Rugby players are just as competitive off the pitch as they are on it, with almost as much kudos to be gained from winning a post-match drinking contest as from scoring a try mid-game.

After a few drinks, there are sometimes a few songs. Ideally these will have an easy-to-learn chorus and a few lewd and innuendo-laden verses for the more seasoned club members to perform. Songs are handed down from generation to generation and in less politically correct times songbooks and albums were published to celebrate the genre of the rude rugby song.

# THE CLUBHOUSE

Rugby players will often display a 'fine disregard' for the normal rules of social decorum. When the French president Georges Pompidou was making a speech at the post-match banquet after France had beaten Wales in 1973, the players persuaded the local town band to march in playing their instruments and bring the rather tedious oration to a premature end.

Elaborate games have been developed in rugby clubhouses solely for the purpose of encouraging more drinking, and games involving rules that become more incomprehensible as the evening wears on have evolved to trap the unwary into a desperately drunken evening. Fortunately for the players' livers, and for the safety of the clubhouse fixtures and fittings, a greater adherence to drink-driving rules over recent decades has probably led to a decline in the greater excesses of rugby clubs. But beneath the surface of every club lies a very messy evening just waiting to happen.

# ALL STADIUMS
# GREAT AND SMALL

•••••••••••••••••••••••••••••••••••••••••••••••••

*" The player's changing room at Twickenham
was as inspiring as a prison cell. Bare, grey
breeze-block walls, a lone unpolished wooden
bench underneath a row of wooden pegs. "*

**CLIVE WOODWARD, ENGLAND RUGBY PLAYER AND COACH**

As the game of rugby grew in popularity, bigger and better
stadiums were needed. International rugby unions have found
the resources to create spectacular settings on which to stage
some very special sporting moments and the supporters, with
their own particular approach to the art of spectating, have also
played their part in making the game what it is today.

Unlike the association game, with its segregated stands and
the ever-present threat of violence breaking out on the terraces
and sometimes even on the pitch, rugby terraces have tended
to be far more affable environments. Fans of opposing sides
are seated together and might engage in a little good-natured
banter, but rarely anything more serious. Fans are also mostly

trusted to enjoy an alcoholic drink or two as they watch the game.

At the same time, of course, there was still an important role played by the smaller clubhouses. Many have had to get creative and improvise in order to survive. All have their own traditions, quirks and particular charm, and they all have an important role to play in maintaining the reach of the game into communities all around the country. Whatever the attractions of the grand stages, many fans and players still enjoy the familiarity, friendship and family atmosphere of the smaller local clubs.

Whatever the size of the venue, though, the rituals of the journey to the ground are as important as the game itself: the pre-match breakfast, the train or car journey to the ground, a pint or two nearby and a spot of lunch, and the final walk to the ground with fellow fans as the atmosphere builds.

## ELLIS PARK STADIUM, JOHANNESBURG

This stadium has been home to the Springboks since 1928 and hosted the 1995 Rugby World Cup final, where the new, post-apartheid South Africa, with President Mandela watching in the stands, beat New Zealand. This was the first ever rugby international to require a period of extra time, with the sides level at 9–9 after 80 minutes. After the first ten-minute period of extra time both sides were still level, having exchanged penalties at 12–12. It was then, with just seven minutes to go, that Joel Stransky drop-kicked the goal that gave South Africa a 15–12 win, and gave a beaming Nelson Mandela the task of handing the Webb Ellis Cup to the Springboks' captain Francois Pienaar.

## VIGO RFC, MEOPHAM, KENT

Of course it is not essential to have a massive stadium to enjoy your rugby. One club was launched at the end of the 1968 season after a well-lubricated Sunday lunch in a Kent pub, when the landlady of the Vigo Inn offered to lend some of her regulars a field on which to play. The club was christened Vigo RFC and set about trying to work out how to finance a set of posts. After their initial fundraising efforts came to nothing, some diseased elms from a nearby forest were chopped down and fashioned into a set of posts. For many years there was no clubhouse and the players would change in the public bar. This was back in the days of licensing laws that meant pubs had to close during the afternoons. However, if the landlady was indisposed, the players had to use a chicken shed in the corner of the field instead. After the match, each Vigo player would take home a visiting opponent, run him a bath, give him a cup of tea and something to eat and escort him back to the pub for a pint and a singsong. The pub on the A227 became a bit of a tourist attraction as a result.

In later years the club moved to a local village hall, constructing a five-man, L-shaped bath in a back room. Players had to trudge back along a one-mile walk to reach the playing field until a kindly local dame gifted the club some land that had been earmarked for the purposes of recreation. The stones and the sheep on the field were cleared and club members set about erecting a brand-new clubhouse, drafting in family and friends to help with the construction. The club survives to this day with four senior sides and thriving mini and junior sections.

# MURRAYFIELD STADIUM, EDINBURGH

Murrayfield is the largest sports arena of any sort in Scotland and has been home to the Scottish national side and the Edinburgh club side since March 1925.

In the days before all-seater stadiums, Murrayfield hosted its biggest crowd at a rugby match when 104,000 fans watched Scotland play Wales. With modern seating in place, the capacity is now 67,130.

In 2007 Scotland played host to the Azzurri of Italy at Murrayfield. After just 1 minute and 14 seconds the Italian centre Mirco Bergamasco had charged down a Scotland kick, picked up the ball and scored the opening try. Minutes later

Andrea Scanavacca intercepted a pass from Scottish scrum half Chris Cusiter and shot off to score another try; Italian winger Kaine Robertson then ran from halfway to score. With three tries and a 21–0 lead after just 5 minutes, Italy had achieved a spectacular start and one that only the All Blacks had ever managed before.

## SOUTHWOLD RFC, SUFFOLK

Southwold Rugby Club was founded in 1964 and its members applied to the local council for permission to use part of Southwold Common as a pitch. The council duly obliged and space was found on the large piece of land between the harbour and the town. The common already had a nine-hole golf course, a cricket and a football pitch when rugby was added to the local sports offering. Southwold's Harbour Inn was requisitioned as a changing room, clubhouse and venue for post-match teas.

Not everyone in the local area was entirely happy about the placing of a rugby pitch on an area criss-crossed with ancient pathways. During the club's first season an elderly lady decided to exercise her right of way to walk, with her dog, diagonally across the pitch during home fixtures. This soon became part of the club folklore. Referees and opposition teams were warned in advance and play was stopped when the elderly lady made her appearance. She would be welcomed with a polite 'Good afternoon' from the players and applauded from the pitch. This continued for a few seasons before the lady concerned passed away.

# MILLENNIUM STADIUM, CARDIFF

Opened, as the name suggests, in time for the millennium celebrations, this ground is shared with the Welsh national football team and is the second-largest rugby stadium in the world. With a fully retractable roof and a capacity of 74,500, in 2013 it was the stage for Wales's biggest ever win over England when the Welsh team crushed English hopes of a Grand Slam, beating them by 30–3 and winning the Six Nations tournament. With 70,000 Welsh fans chanting 'Easy, easy,' it was a miserable day for England, ending the new coach Stuart Lancaster's early winning run.

# RACAL DECCA RFC, TOLWORTH, SURREY

Back in the 1950s and 1960s a number of businesses realised that sport generally was a great way of building company loyalty and camaraderie, and a large number formed sports and social clubs for their employees. One such was the Decca Company, the record business that famously turned down the Beatles. In 1959 a rugby section was formed and started playing fixtures against other local sides from their base at Tolworth in Surrey. Club membership was limited to employees of the firm, although guests were allowed to play occasionally but couldn't buy drinks from the bar, yet still had to pay an entrance fee for the privilege. The company and the club changed their name in 1979 to Racal Decca following a takeover by an electronics business, and the rugby club became open to all comers. Eventually the social club declined and the clubhouse was sold and redeveloped, but somehow the rugby club has survived.

Racal Decca now claim to be the world's smallest rugby club. So proud are they of their diminutive status that in 2015, whilst the world's biggest international teams were travelling to England for the Rugby World Cup, they staged their very own Small Clubs World Cup. They invited clubs with just a single side to join them in Tolworth on 19 September and booked out the Kingston University changing facilities for their visitors. Twelve teams entered the competition, including clubs from Wales and Malta. After a joyous day, with a guest appearance from the England World Cup-winning coach Clive Woodward, Cambridge-based Cottingham Renegades were presented with the winners' trophy by the England Women's World Cup winner La Toya Mason.

Racal Decca seem to have the right idea about player recruitment. As their skipper Sean Phelan said to the

*Wandsworth Guardian*, 'We are always looking for bright new talent. However, we are also delighted to get stale old talent too.'

## STADE DE FRANCE, PARIS

The Stade de France was built for the 1998 football World Cup and is used by the national football and rugby teams. It is also used occasionally by Stade Français, the Parisian side that plays in bright-pink shirts, as well as Racing Metro, the other rugby club in Paris, which opts for a kit of baby blue and white hoops.

With a capacity of 81,338, it is the only stadium in the world to have hosted a World Cup final in both rugby and the association game. Sadly for the French, however, they didn't get to play in the 2007 Rugby World Cup final in their nation's capital, having been knocked out by England in the semis.

## STREATHAM-CROYDON RFC, SOUTH LONDON

If you were walking, cycling or driving along Brigstock Road towards Thornton Heath in south London, you could be forgiven for not noticing a rugby club in what would otherwise appear to be an ordinary urban street. But careful inspection of one of the Victorian, double-fronted houses reveals a small sign above the front door between the two bay windows welcoming you to Streatham-Croydon Rugby Club. Knock on the door and you would be welcomed into what once would have been a living room but is now a rugby club bar. If you are lucky you might arrive just as the favoured post-match tea of this long-established local club – a tray of roast potatoes – is coming out of the oven.

Streatham-Croydon claims to be the fifth-oldest club in England, formed in 1871. The club moved to its current ground just after the First World War, after its original pitches had been cut up and given over to the vital war work of growing vegetables. A cricket pitch behind Brigstock Road became available and was acquired with a loan from the RFU. The house at 159 Brigstock Road was purchased in 1921 and converted into a clubhouse with a tearoom, bar and showers. This was a huge improvement on the facilities that had been on offer at the Prince of Wales public house which had served as a headquarters up until that point.

During the 1960s the club regularly ran 12 sides but demographic changes in the local area led to a decline in the numbers playing at the club and the senior side gradually slipped down the leagues. In the late 1990s and early 2000s the club was struggling at times to put out a single side, until they adopted an active programme of engaging with the new communities that were moving in and creating a vibrant and ethnically diverse neighbourhood. The club has worked hard to break down cultural and religious barriers and is welcoming to all sectors of the community. Gang members, former prisoners on rehabilitation programmes and asylum seekers have all become regular members and the club has helped many change their lives for the better. The club now has become more than just a rugby club. It's now a community hub that breaks down stereotypes and brings people together – and the roast potatoes are delicious!

# TWICKENHAM STADIUM, LONDON

Back in 1907, this former market garden was purchased by the RFU for £5,572 12s 6d. It is still occasionally referred to as Billy's Cabbage Patch after Billy Williams, the RFU committee member who made the original investment.

The stadium was opened in 1909 and has been English Rugby's headquarters ever since. The South Stand was demolished in 2005 and rebuilt, increasing the total capacity to 82,000.

Twickenham holds the honour of having been the stage for the first streaker to bare all in front of thousands at a sporting event. Michael O'Brien stripped off for a bet and ran across the pitch in 1974 during an England–Wales fixture. A young officer, PC Perry, caught up with him and, making good use of his policeman's helmet to hide any embarrassment, escorted O'Brien from the ground. Speaking to *The Guardian* in 2006, Perry said, 'It was a cold day and he didn't have anything to be proud of. We took him to the nick but he was back for the second half.'

## DARLINGTON MOWDEN PARK RUGBY CLUB, DURHAM

Every rugby fan will be familiar with Twickenham Stadium, but not many would be able to name the second-largest stadium in England used exclusively for rugby union. The Darlington Arena has that accolade, with a capacity of 25,000, and is home to Darlington Mowden Park Rugby Club. The only problem is that on most match days the first team plays in front of at least 24,000 empty seats.

Still, the club aren't complaining. They acquired the impressive ground for a knockdown price after the local football club's owner was arrested for money laundering and declared bankrupt. The football club sank out of the football league and the local rugby club stepped in to take its place in the town. First-team player Ross Doneghan told the BBC that he feels proud to play in such an impressive setting and that, 'We're not thinking about the empty seats. We're thinking about the game.'

The enterprising rugby club somehow manage to cover the running costs of their massive venue by hiring out the facilities for weddings and corporate functions whenever they can. Most clubhouses at their level would have a couple of rooms and a bar. Darlington's stadium is a little grander than that, with escalators transporting fans between function rooms on different levels. The club are determined to find new ways to realise the full potential of the stadium and make the most of this fortuitous acquisition from their friends in the association game.

## STADIUM AUSTRALIA, SYDNEY

Built for the Sydney Olympics in 2000, Stadium Australia managed to squeeze in some six-figure crowds for a few fixtures before whittling its capacity down to 83,500 by lopping off a tier or two and moving some lower stands closer to the action.

Stadium Australia has the unusual ability to morph from a rectangular pitch for rugby union, rugby league and the occasional football match into an oval one for playing Aussie rules.

In 2013 the ground, now known for sponsorship reasons as the ANZ Stadium, hosted the final and deciding Test of the British and Irish Lions tour. The team from the British Isles were desperately looking for their first series win in 16 years and the first two Tests had been nail-bitingly close, with England having won the first Test by just two points and Australia having won the second Test by only one point. The former Welsh national side coach Warren Gatland had made six changes to the Lions side that lost the second Test, controversially dropping Irish star centre Brian O'Driscoll from a starting line-up that included ten Welsh players. In the end Gatland was proved right as the Lions won convincingly by 41 points to 16, with Welsh full back and player of the series Leigh Halfpenny kicking 21 of them through the posts.

# THE SPIRIT OF THE GAME

·················································

*A man who plays it must be ready to give and take hard knocks but he will give and take them with a grin.*
**FROM *RUGGER*, W. WAKEFIELD AND H. MARSHALL, 1930**

At the end of many a game of rugby, players, spectators and commentators talk among themselves about the 'spirit' in which the game was played and whether or not it was the right one. A game played in the right spirit is one where the contest is uncompromising, tough, aggressive and physical, quite often played with a real anger and heartfelt loathing of your opposite number. However, immediately after the final whistle is blown, players on all sides will show the utmost respect, affection and genuine friendship towards their opponents. Indeed, the harder the game is played, the greater the degree of respect that is given.

The spirit of rugby draws heavily on the ancient codes of chivalry by which knights of old would do battle within a set of rules designed to ensure a fair fight. Victory would be sought not at all costs, but with honour. Much the same set of codes applies to rugby. There is an expectation that you will play with a certain degree of ferocity and animosity. To do less than that would in itself be disrespectful to your opponent. Whether you win or lose, a team that plays its rugby in the right spirit will be invited back year after year for another match.

Very rarely will you see a rugby player feign injury in order to trick a referee into punishing an opposite player. Not for rugby the histrionics and Oscar-winning performances associated with the association game. More often than not a rugby player will keep quiet about any stray punch or shoeing that he or she might have received. Far better to keep an opponent on the pitch where you or your teammates can exact some sort of revenge than to see him sent off to the safety of the clubhouse and a warm bath.

Quite often, too, a player will accept, maybe not cheerfully but certainly stoically, any revenge that might be exacted upon them. Many a player will be heard to say that they probably deserved the shoeing or slap that followed a particular misdemeanour. The team captains resolved disputes in the very earliest games; today many a minor dispute is still resolved between players without any need for a referee or assistant referee to get involved.

The spirit of rugby is often beautifully encapsulated within literature and music, some instances of which we will now look at in this chapter.

## RUGBY IN LITERATURE

Perhaps it is not surprising that rugby, having been created in a seat of learning, should also inspire some great literature. The game of rugby itself has such a powerful narrative that it has led to some great reads.

## *TOM BROWN'S SCHOOL DAYS* – THOMAS HUGHES, 1857

Thomas Hughes's semi-autobiographical novel of 1857 is set at Rugby School and was originally published as having been written by 'an old boy of Rugby'. The character of Tom Brown is based on Hughes's brother George and, amid tales of bullying and cruelty, is a description of Tom's early experience of finding himself at the bottom of a ruck in the middle of a game on the school playing fields:

> *They are hauled off and roll off him, and Tom is discovered a motionless body. Old Brooke picks him up. 'Stand back, give him air,' he says and then feeling his limbs, adds, 'No bones broken. How do you feel, young un?' 'Hah-hah,' gasps Tom as his wind comes back, 'pretty well, thank you – all right.' 'Who is he?' says Brooke. 'Oh, it's Brown, he's a new boy; I know him,' says East, coming up. 'Well, he is a plucky youngster, and will make a player,' says Brooke.*

## 'THE ADVENTURE OF THE SUSSEX VAMPIRE' – ARTHUR CONAN DOYLE, 1924

In this Sherlock Holmes tale published in 1924 we discover the key fact in Dr Watson's backstory that perhaps best describes his loyal, resourceful and determined nature. Watson previously played rugby for Blackheath.

## *CASTLE GAY* – JOHN BUCHAN, 1930

John Buchan may be better known for giving the world *The Thirty-Nine Steps*, but he also made a useful contribution to the rugby literary canon. *Castle Gay* is a tale of the self-discovery of a media mogul named Craw, overseen by Jaikie Galt, an international rugby player. They travel around the Scottish wilderness re-evaluating their lives and values and coming to differing conclusions.

### HOW GREEN WAS MY VALLEY – RICHARD LLEWELLYN, 1939

Set in the mining village of Gilfach Goch near Tonypandy, Llewellyn's 1939 novel offers perhaps the most poetic description anywhere of what happens in Wales when a fly half fails to get rid of the ball quickly enough and, being greedy to score a try himself rather than pass to his wing, tries to sell a dummy to his opponent, Cyfartha:

> **❝** *... and how the crowd is laughing now, for to sell a dummy to Cyfartha is to sell poison to a Borgia...* **❞**

### A STORY – DYLAN THOMAS, 1953

Thomas's tale of a young boy from west Wales travelling with a group of men on a drunken journey to Porthcawl contains a delightful gem of rugby-related dialogue, or what might have passed for banter in those days, between Enoch Davies and 'a stranger' who claims to have played for Aberavon in 1898. Davies calls him a liar; when the stranger says he can show him photos, Davies says they must be forged; when he offers to show him his cap, he says it must be stolen. Finally the stranger, furious, says he has friends to back him up. 'Bribed,' says Enoch Davies.

### WORK, SEX AND RUGBY – LEWIS DAVIES, 1998

This book from 1998 describing one man's odyssey through a weekend of drinking, rugby and women was voted the best book to describe Wales by the World Book Day campaign to encourage more reading, particularly among young men.

# THE MUSIC OF RUGBY

Part of the warm-up ritual for supporters and players alike is a little clearing of the windpipes and a spot of communal singing, and rugby has become associated with some great anthems and inspired composers to pen yet more tunes.

### 'CWM RHONDDA' – JOHN HUGHES, 1905

Also known as the 'Welsh Rugby Hymn', 'Cwm Rhondda' is the tune written by John Hughes as a setting for the words of William Williams's 'Guide Me, O Thou Great Redeemer'. Sung whenever Wales are playing, it is one of the few tunes where the terrace choirs split into two parts, with one section repeating the last three syllables of the penultimate line of each verse e.g. 'want no more' or 'strength and shield'. The tradition of Welsh male voice choirs means that this is probably the most tunefully rendered anthem of any rugby fixture. Annoyingly, football fans have stolen the music for their own somewhat less elegant chant, 'You're not singing anymore.'

### RUGBY (SYMPHONIC MOVEMENT NO. 2) – ARTHUR HONEGGER, 1928

The Swiss composer, born in France, was inspired to produce his second symphonic movement while watching the rugby in the

Colombes stadium in Paris, home of the Racing Metro rugby club. This is how he described the difference between rugby and football:

> **❝** *I very much like the game of football, but I prefer rugby. I find it more spontaneous, more direct and closer to nature than football, which is a more scientific game. For me the savage, brusque, untidy and desperate rhythm of rugby is more attractive.* **❞**

## 'THE WORLD IN UNION' – LYRICS BY CHARLIE SKARBEK, 1991

This was commissioned, no doubt with the best of intentions, by a committee of the International Rugby Board. It borrows the tune from the powerful and moving hymn 'I Vow to Thee My Country', which in turn borrows its tune from Holst's 'Jupiter' from *The Planets*. Skarbek makes a brave but not entirely successful attempt with his lyrics to capture the spirit of international friendship that pervades rugby union. To be honest, it is only brought out every four years at the World Cup, listened to politely at the opening ceremony and then quietly forgotten once the proper community singing and the Haka take over.

## 'SWING LOW, SWEET CHARIOT' – WALLACE WILLIS, PRIOR TO 1862

It was, of course, those public schoolboys who would give English rugby its finest anthem. In the last game of the 1988 season, a group of boys from the Benedictine Douai School in Woolhampton, Berkshire, were at Twickenham to watch the game against Ireland. Under the guidance of Benedictine monks the school first XV had adopted the hymn 'Swing Low, Sweet Chariot' and the schoolboys began to sing their team song from the stands. Nigerian-born winger Chris Oti was having a great game that day and the schoolboys sang with particular enthusiasm each time he got the ball. In the end Oti had run in a hat-trick of tries and the England supporters had a new anthem that would travel the world with them.

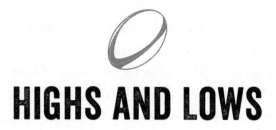

# HIGHS AND LOWS

Rugby has had its fair share of ups and downs, some days that have made everyone smile from ear to cauliflower ear, and others when it has had rugby fans and players alike feeling embarrassed and ashamed. Good or bad, these stories highlight the values that the sport holds dear.

This chapter contains a selection of some of rugby's triumphs and disasters for your reading pleasure (or not, as the case may be).

## THE TWICKENHAM STREAKER

In January 1982, the Twickenham Streaker, otherwise known as Erika Roe, shot to fame during an England v Australia Test match. Apparently the young and well-endowed Erika hadn't been planning to go to the game and was supposed to be at work in a bookshop in Petersfield, but was jollied into travelling by her older sister Sally. Along with a group of about 25 rugby fans they arrived at Twickenham and headed straight for the beer tent.

To avoid the attentions of a lecherous companion, Erika and a friend moved to the front of the stand, but by half time were getting a little restless. Speaking to *The Observer* in 2001, Erika said, 'We were getting a bit bored, thought we should do something and within seconds had decided, "Let's streak."'

After passing her bra and packet of Marlboro cigarettes to some people behind her she set off onto the pitch, to huge cheers from the crowd. Eventually a policeman caught up with her and did his best to protect her modesty.

After a few public appearances and modelling offers from *Playboy* and *The Sun* she gradually retreated into relative obscurity. In 2011, though, she decided to use her particular fame to raise money for Breast Cancer Research, after her sister died from the disease. Her daughter Imogen, a fine art student, put together a calendar of images of her mum and the money raised was donated to the charity.

# WOODEN SPOON

Heroic failure is still celebrated in rugby and in 1983 led to the founding of a children's charity, called Wooden Spoon.

As England picked up the title after a dismal Six Nations campaign, a small group of travelling England supporters were ceremoniously awarded a real wooden spoon by a group of Irish fans. A charity golf match followed to see which of the fans would have the honour of keeping the spoon. The money raised paid for a school minibus and the charity was born.

The charity now has a few staff in an office in Surrey, 40 regional committees and 11,000 members, and has handed out over £12 million to good causes.

# EAR TODAY...

In 1994 the All Blacks rugby team were hosting South Africa in a three-match Test series. Following a 13–9 victory in the second Test in Wellington, the All Blacks clinched the series, but the game would be remembered for more than their victory.

During the game the All Blacks' captain Sean Fitzpatrick told referee Brian Stirling that he had had his ear bitten. Stirling and his touch judges hadn't seen the incident, which took place during a ruck, so no action was taken during the game. But the culprit wasn't about to get away with it: TV cameras had recorded South African prop Johan le Roux biting Fitzpatrick's ear.

Le Roux – nicknamed 'The Beast' – was sent home in disgrace and banned for 18 months. He missed the World Cup, which was won by his own country. He said: 'For an 18-month suspension,

I feel I probably should have torn it off. Then at least I could say: "Look, I've returned to South Africa with the guy's ear."'

Le Roux had previous form when it came to dishing out on-field pain. A couple of months before his nibble at Fitzpatrick's ear, he had put England player Martin Johnson out of action with one punch. Fearing concussion, Johnson flew home and was replaced on the tour.

After his 18-month suspension was up, le Roux returned to playing and in his second match back was suspended for seven weeks after headbutting an opponent.

# POISONED

The Rugby Union World Cup final of 1995 was held at Ellis Park, Johannesburg, where host country South Africa met the All Blacks. President Nelson Mandela was in attendance at the final, his symbolic wearing of a South African jersey showing his desire for reconciliation in the once-divided nation. The All Blacks were favourites to lift the Webb Ellis Cup, with Jonah Lomu in dynamic form. In the semi-final against England he had scored four tries as his team notched a 45–29 victory.

In a close game, South Africa gained the vital advantage with a drop goal in extra time, the final score being 15–12. However, during the game some of the All Blacks were seen vomiting at the side of the pitch, and after the match was over it was revealed that 26 of the All Blacks' 37-strong party had suffered from food poisoning before the game. They had kept it quiet so as not to give the South Africans the advantage of knowing their opponents were in a weakened state.

The New Zealand coach, Laurie Mains, claimed that a waitress called Suzie had poisoned water given to the team and that the poisoning was a deliberate act to spoil the All Blacks' chances in the final. No evidence was found of a conspiracy and 'Suzie' was never located – but in 2000, Rory Steyn, the South African who was in charge of the security for the team, wrote in his autobiography, 'There is no doubt that the All Blacks were poisoned two days before the final.'

The team's manager, Colin Meads, thought the source of the illness might be milk that was off. The team's doctor, Mike Bowen, thought that urns containing tea and coffee had been tampered with. He said, 'It was unlikely to have been something that occurred incidentally or without some provocation, but I have no way of proving that was the case.'

As if the illness hadn't left a bad enough taste in the New Zealanders' mouths, there was more to come in the formal dinner to mark the end of the tournament. South African Rugby president Louis Luyt made a speech in which he said, 'There were no true world champions in the 1987 and 1991 World Cups because South Africa were not there. We have proved our point.'

New Zealand had won the 1987 competition. The team got up and walked out, and the English and French parties joined them.

# RUGBY ROMANCE

Wills and Kate aren't the only couple to have found romance in the remote Scottish university of St Andrews. Nikki and Euan Isles found each other there and it was the addition of rugby that brought a spark to their relationship. In a real-life parallel to the film *Bend It Like Beckham*, Nikki was the captain of the women's rugby side and Euan was their coach. It was on a rugby night out in 1999 that they decided to get together and six years later they were married. Speaking to the *Daily Record*, Nikki said, 'I never thought I would meet Mr Right on a rugby pitch... I found the perfect husband.'

# RECORD-BREAKING START

It's always satisfying when a plan comes together and for the Scottish Test side playing Wales at Murrayfield in February 1999 their plan came together rather quickly as they scored international rugby's fastest ever try.

While several spectators were still finding their seats, the two sides lined up for the kick-off with the Scottish forwards lined up on the right-hand side of the pitch in a fairly conventional-looking starting position. However, just before the kick-off Scotland's fly half Duncan Hodge switched round and kicked the ball to the more sparsely populated left-hand side of the pitch. Now this sort of tactic is more often used by desperate amateur sides facing an oversized opposition pack at the end of a game when they are already several points down and desperate to try anything that might get them onto the scoreboard.

Scotland's game plan was to target the Welsh back Matthew Robinson and put him under pressure from the start. Robinson was one of only two defenders on the left-hand side of the pitch, playing alongside Shane Howarth at the kick-off. Howarth rushed ahead of Robinson to claim the ball but was immediately set upon by Scottish centre John Leslie. The speedy and powerful son of a former All Blacks captain, Leslie quickly ripped the ball from Howarth's grasp and set off for the Welsh line. Within seconds Scotland were five points up and the press corps were frantically looking at their watches to see if the previous record of 10 seconds set by England against Wales in 1923 had been broken. Careful scrutiny of the BBC replays at half time revealed that the ball had been grounded just 9 seconds after the referee's whistle had been blown and a new record was established. The game continued at much the same pace for the remaining 79 minutes and 51 seconds, with Scotland emerging victorious at the end by 33 points to 20.

## DALLAGLIO AND THE WRONG SORT OF WHITE LINES

In 1999 England rugby captain Lawrence Dallaglio was embroiled in a scandal when a newspaper alleged he had both used and sold drugs before he played rugby. He was also reported to have celebrated the British and Irish Lions' victory in South Africa in 1997 by taking ecstasy and cocaine. The England captain strenuously denied the story and said it was a set-up. His mother backed him, saying, 'If my son took drugs, then I would know about it. He has always been a level-headed boy.'

The *News of the World* stood by their story, with editor Phil Hall saying, 'We are amazed at his denial.' Dallaglio resigned the captaincy the day after the story broke, following a meeting with the Rugby Football Union. After an investigation was carried out he was fined £15,000 for bringing the game into disrepute. Dallaglio later regained the captaincy.

# A GREAT WELSH COMEBACK

The year 1999 was a big one for Wales. At the same time as the first set of elections were being held for the newly formed Welsh Assembly, a spectacular new national stadium was emerging in Cardiff, and massive Welsh bands like Catatonia, Stereophonics and Manic Street Preachers were topping the charts and soundtracking the year for a generation. Some have argued it was the year that defined modern Wales. It was also the year of one of Welsh rugby's greatest ever comebacks.

Fresh from an emotional defeat of England in the last ever Five Nations international, Wales and their New Zealand coach Graham Henry headed for a tour of Argentina to prepare for the Rugby World Cup. Things started to go wrong, however, as they were heading to the ground for their first Test fixture against the Pumas. Horrendous Buenos Aires traffic and a police escort that failed to show up meant they arrived at the pitch with barely 40 minutes to spare. Amateur club players will be all too familiar with this sort of scenario, but international players tend to like a little more time to prepare for their games. A flustered Welsh side slumped to a 23-point deficit as they failed to put any score on the board during the first half hour.

Fortunately, though, the Welsh team's new Kiwi coach had instilled in his squad a strong dose of courage and grit. After one successful penalty kick from Neil Jenkins to get the scoreboard ticking over, Dafydd James sprinted in for a try on the stroke of half time that did much to restore Welsh morale. As they headed for the changing room and the half-time oranges, there was still a huge task ahead of the Welsh. The previous biggest ever comeback in a Test match was when the Springboks had reversed an 18-point deficit to beat the All Blacks a year earlier. Now the second half was dominated by a resurgent Welsh pack, with two tries coming from lineouts. The first was by Brett Sinkinson and the second was from Chris Wyatt, who charged over the line after brilliant runs from the Welsh centres. Consistent and accurate kicking from Neil Jenkins helped keep the scoreboard ticking over and in the end the Welsh finished the game with 36 points to Argentina's 26.

Wales went on to host a hugely successful World Cup in the autumn and the nation saw off the old millennium with a massive concert in their new Millennium Stadium with the Manics, Feeder and the Super Furry Animals playing to a crowd of 57,000.

# RUGBY REACHES WAR-TORN RWANDA

In 1994 Rwanda was devastated by one of the most horrific acts of genocide, when 800,000 people were killed over 100 days of violence between Hutus and Tutsis. After a slow period of reconciliation and reconstruction a number of international development organisations began to work there to help rebuild the nation.

One such organisation was Voluntary Service Overseas, and one volunteer in 2001 was Emma Rees, an international politics graduate and keen rugby player from Aberystwyth University. On her own as an English teacher in a solely French-speaking village, Emma found settling in initially quite difficult as her French was limited; she also missed playing rugby. So with one rugby ball and a few coloured socks filled with sand to mark out a playing area, Emma introduced her pupils to the game.

At first, when she showed them a video of a rather tough Cardiff game, the children were terrified. However, Rwanda is known as the Land of a Thousand Hills so their natural fitness levels were very high. Emma convinced them to play and they loved it. The game spread quickly among the local children and Emma formed the Federation of Rwandan Rugby to develop the sport. A charity, Friends of Rwandan Rugby, was created shortly afterwards, with rugby legends like Jason Leonard among its patrons. Over the years numerous coaches and players from overseas have travelled to Rwanda to teach the game and help young people make new friends through the sport.

Rwanda became an associate member of the International Rugby Board in 2004 and a full member in 2015. Its national side, the Silverbacks, compete in one of the lower divisions of the Africa Cup against Burundi, Lesotho and the Democratic Republic of Congo. The Rwanda Rugby Federation has ten teams competing in a national 15-a-side league with more than 300 registered adult male players, 60 adult female players and 7,000 youth players. Thanks to one rugby-mad girl from Aberystwyth, the game continues to grow and create new friendships all around the world.

# RED CARPET TREATMENT

When England's rugby team came to Dublin's Lansdowne Road in 2003, a crucial match lay ahead. Either Ireland or England could win the Grand Slam and the Six Nations championship. Ireland were chasing their first Grand Slam in 55 years, while England's last one had been more recent, in 1995.

The battle began before a ball had even been kicked or carried, as England captain Martin Johnson found himself getting into a bad mood. Never a fan of the jobsworth busybodies that lurk around the fringes of international fixtures, he had been particularly irritated by an Irish blazer-wearing hanger-on with a clipboard pestering him for a signature before the game. As he led his team out, he made his players line up in front of the red carpet – which turned out to be the area where the home side would normally stand. Johnno had failed to read the four-page etiquette document for visiting teams on match days. Despite being invited to move along, Johnson refused to budge. He had Neil Back standing next to him saying, 'No Johnno, you can't concede on this. Don't concede... don't concede.' The Irish side, rather than standing in front of the other stretch of red carpet that had been set aside for the English, chose to line up further to the right of Johnson's men on the grass. This meant that the VIP being presented to the teams – Ireland's president Mary McAleese – had to shake hands while walking across the turf rather than the comfy Axminster that had been rolled out for this purpose.

Commentators afterwards credited Johnno's 'gamesmanship' with giving his side the psychological edge that enabled them to secure a victory by 42 points to 6. Johnson later claimed it was an innocent mistake, combined perhaps with a 'deep-rooted dislike of petty officials'.

# BORN TOULOUSE

Rugby is a game where the occasional fist being thrown isn't regarded as anything untoward. It's a different matter when the fists are thrown at spectators.

Irishman Trevor Brennan was a forward for French club Toulouse when his team faced Ulster at home in the Heineken Cup on 21 January 2007. He had started his career at a junior club in Dublin, which led to his nickname 'the Barnhall Bruiser'.

Brennan was a substitute for the game and in the second half was warming up on the touchline. There was some good-natured banter with some of the crowd, then things turned nasty. Brennan went over the perimeter wall towards the crowd. The 6 ft 5 in. player went up some stairs and then started laying into an Ulster fan, Patrick Bamford, hitting him six or seven times, leaving him bruised and shaken.

Brennan claimed he had been subjected to abuse about his mother and also sectarian comments from the crowd, but an inquiry found this not to be the case. The Ulster fans had been slagging off the bar he owned in Toulouse, with Bamford shouting that the bar was 'crap'.

After the altercation Brennan was led away but still took part in the game, yet soon after was sin-binned for fighting with Ulster's Justin Harrison. He was later fined €25,000 and given a lifetime ban from playing the game and from participating in any capacity in European Cup games, although this was later reduced to five years. He was also ordered to pay €5,000 in damages to Bamford and was fined €800 by French criminal authorities. The 33-year-old had retired from rugby before the punishments were announced.


# BLOODGATE

On 12 April 2009 the English Premiership side Harlequins were playing Leinster at the Twickenham Stoop in the quarter-finals of the Heineken Cup, the tournament that pits the very best European club sides against each other. With a place in the semi-finals at stake, Harlequins were behind by just one point with ten minutes to play. What happened next was effectively to end the career of one of the all-time rugby greats and introduce a new '-gate' to the list of media scandals.

Substitute winger Tom Williams came on, replacing the injured fly half Chris Malone, who had previously come on as a replacement for Nigel Evans. This left Quins without a recognised kicker on the pitch and desperate for just two or three last-minute points, perhaps from a penalty or a drop kick.

Someone somewhere then came up with the idea of getting the specialist kicker Evans back on the field, but the only way to do that would be for him to come on as a temporary blood replacement. A blood capsule was smuggled into the mouth of Tom Williams and he came off with a wink for his teammates, captured by a Sky TV cameraman.

Complaints and inquiries followed, revealing that a doctor had later deliberately cut Williams' mouth in order to make the fake injury a real one. Dean Richards, the legendary former England and Lions number 8 and Harlequins director of rugby, was given a three-year ban from having anything to do with the sport. Tom Williams had an initial 12-month ban reduced to four for co-operating with the authorities in the inquiry. Harlequins were fined just over a quarter of a million pounds.

Dean Richards said afterwards, 'I took full responsibility for it. It was a farcical situation, it really was. It didn't pan out particularly well on the day.'

## ANDY POWELL AND THE GOLF BUGGY

Welsh international back-row forward Andy Powell may not have been the greatest ever player to pull on a red shirt for his country, but he has certainly played an important role in some of the post-match celebrations.

In the small hours of 13 February 2010, he was celebrating hard with his teammates after a dramatic victory against Scotland in the Six Nations tournament, where they had scored 17 points in the final five minutes to win. For some reason, in what can only be forwards' logic, he decided that a golf buggy would be the perfect vehicle for a quick trip to a service station for 'munchies'. Powell drove a mile and a half along the M4 before being stopped by police and breathalysed.

In court, Powell's lawyer said, 'Beer is a staple of any rugby side and here there was more than a few pints of beer... As soon as the police arrived, he realised he had made a mistake and without hesitation he accepted blame.'

According to the prosecuting lawyer, what he actually said to the police was 'I'm an idiot, I know. Going down the M4 in a golf buggy, I'm a professional rugby player. What have I done?'

Naturally, and quite rightly, Powell was banned from driving and dropped from the international side, but he gave a few traffic police officers and sports reporters a laugh or two as they attempted to piece together the events following the night's celebrations.


## DWARF TOSSING

When a team's management are deciding whether or not to allow their players a night out during a major tournament away from home, several factors have to be considered. If they ban nights out they could have on their hands a group of disgruntled players cooped up in a hotel. However, if they let them out and things get out of hand they run the risk of courting bad publicity. The latter happened to England in 2011 at the Rugby World Cup in New Zealand.

England had beaten Argentina in their first game and manager Martin Johnson allowed his players a chance to let off some steam, so they went for a night out in Queenstown. A bar they visited was holding a 'Mad Midget Weekender', although allegations that the team indulged in dwarf-tossing were denied by the players and the bar's manager. Later the same evening Mike Tindall, England's captain, was filmed via CCTV speaking to a woman who wasn't his wife. (Seven weeks previously he had married the Queen's granddaughter Zara Phillips, daughter of Princess Anne.) The footage was leaked to the press and caused a rumpus.

While this wasn't particularly terrible, Tindall had made matters worse by changing his initial version of events. First he claimed he'd returned to the team's hotel on his own, but he had actually gone to another bar with the woman, Jessica Palmer. Matters weren't improved for the England captain when it was revealed that he had once been in a relationship with her. Tindall apologised and was later fined £25,000 and thrown out of the England team's Elite Player Squad, although this fine was later reduced to £15,000 and he was reinstated to the squad on appeal.

This wasn't the end of England's travails. Following their exit from the tournament, there was further trouble when centre Manu Tuilagi jumped from a ferry about to dock in Auckland and swam to the quayside in his underwear. He was fined £3,000 and given a warning by the police. Martin

Johnson stated the obvious: 'This was an irresponsible thing to do.'

The competition generated yet more publicity that the team could have done without:

- The team were issued with a warning after the players' shirt numbers started peeling off their shirts in the game against Argentina, thus making it more difficult for the match referee to identify them. A local printing company was blamed for the mishap.

- The strips themselves had been criticised as England chose an all-black design for their away kit, mimicking that of the host's famous jerseys.

- Martin Johnson was criticised for allowing players to go bungee jumping and white-water rafting on their days off.

- Players James Haskell and Chris Ashton were both given suspended fines of £5,000 by the Rugby Football Union for making lewd comments to a hotel staff member.

- Underwear-swimmer Manu Tuilagi was fined £5,000 for wearing an unauthorised mouthguard bearing a sponsor's name.

- Following England's game with Romania, two coaches were issued with bans after they changed the ball for two conversions to be taken by Jonny Wilkinson, without permission from the referee. The rules state that the same ball used to score the try should be used for the resultant conversion. The coaches replaced the try ball with one that was felt to be better for kicking. Kicking coach Dave Alred and fitness coach Paul Stridgeon were suspended by England's RFU for the game against Scotland.

## JOHNNY REDELINGHUYS

Now, there is a general principle accepted throughout the game that, however much they might like to, forwards aren't allowed to kick the ball. It is accepted that, with their heads generally buried in the darker parts of the scrums and their bodies taking the brunt of most of the battering that goes on in the game, they don't really have the composure and temperament for the fine art of aiming the ball precisely into touch or between the goal posts. That pleasure and responsibility is firmly reserved for the backs. This rule particularly applies to the front row.

So it was a rather rare and special moment when, in the 82nd minute of his 50th and final appearance for his national side, Namibian prop Johnny Redelinghuys was handed the ball and the kicking tee. His side had just scored a late consolation try at the end of a fairly hefty defeat at the hands of Argentina in the 2015 Rugby World Cup. Regular kicker Theuns Kotzé relinquished the responsibilities in honour of the front-row forward's significant contribution to the game as the most capped Namibian player of all time. In front of a packed crowd in the King Power Stadium in Leicester, Redelinghuys steadied himself, adopted the classic Jonny Wilkinson pre-kick stance and no doubt visualised the ball flying gracefully through the sticks and into the stand behind. Fortunately, for backs everywhere, the ball barely reached the height of the crossbar and instead clattered into the posts, confirming once and for all that forwards should never be allowed to kick. Still, everyone left the pitch smiling broadly and bearing aloft the not-insubstantial weight of Namibia's favourite and longest-serving prop.

# RUGBY IN ALL ITS FORMS

> *Rugby is neither a man's game nor a woman's game. It is a universal sport that can be enjoyed by anyone with some space and a ball.*
>
> **KATE PORTER, AUSTRALIAN RUGBY PLAYER**

Rugby takes great pride in being a game that everyone can play. It is a game played by men and women, and it keeps evolving, with new versions of the sport springing up all the time. The same principles remain throughout each variety as it seeks to find more ways to allow people to enjoy picking up a ball and running with it.

The full-contact version of rugby is safer and more enjoyable if there is soft ground and rich turf to fall on, which means that during the warmer months of the year when the ground is harder there is less rugby to be found. Former All Black, diplomat and Member of the New Zealand Parliament Chris Laidlaw said, 'Rugby may have many problems, but the gravest is undoubtedly that of the persistence of summer.' So a number of new versions of the sport have been developed precisely to get around that particular concern. Other adaptations have been made to allow wheelchair users to enjoy a version of the sport and one special game has been created just for the backs.

# RUGBY SEVENS

Whisper it very quietly, but rugby sevens might be the next big thing in rugby. Whilst the 15-a-side game is in rude health and has been steadily growing in terms of participation, spectator numbers and international broadcast audiences, the shorter, faster and, some might argue, better-looking version of the game is developing as a significant, distinctive and increasingly successful form of rugby.

Far from being an entirely modern phenomenon, sevens has a long history. The format was invented by a Scottish butcher called Ned Haig, who was attempting to organise a rugby tournament to raise much-needed funds for his club Melrose. Squeezing several 15-a-side games into a single afternoon was impossible, but several shorter seven-a-side games lent themselves well to a one-day tournament. Six sides from the Scottish Borders took part, with a crowd of 1,600 watching the final between Melrose and local rivals Gala. In 1926 the game travelled down south and the Middlesex Sevens were established. A few years later, Rosslyn Park even further south began putting on a sevens competition for local schools.

Sevens, by its very nature, is an easier game to organise, with fewer players and fewer rules. With the huge packs of forwards removed, it is easier to follow and quicker to learn. Sevens is played during the summer on a full-sized pitch, with two halves of just seven minutes each, the scrums consisting of just three players from each side. With fewer players, there is a lot more running around. Some people have suggested that the main reason for organising sevens tournaments is to give the backs a chance to run around and warm up after a long season standing around in the cold waiting for the forwards to release the ball. With the shorter games and typically a tournament format, sevens festivals also lend themselves to a lot of drinking.

On the back of its successful Olympic return in 2016, rugby sevens does look set to grow even further. This prospect does, however, leave those of us who have only ever played the 15-man game, and particularly as front-row forwards enjoying a gentle walk from one scrum to the next, wondering whether we may need to shed a little weight ourselves in order to enjoy this slimmed-down summer version of the sport.

# BEACH RUGBY

Hot on the heels of beach volleyball, a new seaside sporting spectacle is emerging. Since 2006 Swansea has hosted an annual beach rugby tournament which in 2016 attracted 36 teams; although it has to be noted that four of them were expelled during the tournament for brawling on the pitch. International tournaments have also been organised in Italy, France and the USA, and a European Beach Rugby Association oversees the rules and runs a European Series.

Myles Ward, an enterprising young wine dealer, found that he and his friends enjoyed a holiday beach rugby tournament in France so much that in 2013 he decided to reserve a corner of the Covent Garden Piazza in London, order a few lorryloads of sand, find a brewer to sponsor the proceedings and create the first London Beach Rugby tournament. The event proved so successful that he gave up the day job to focus on developing the tournament and taking it to more cities around the world. In 2016 46 teams took part over two days, involving 500 players and 6,000 spectators who between them consumed some 7,500 pints of beer.

The pitches for the London Beach Rugby tournament measure 25 m x 15 m and are surrounded by an inflatable wall. Some 250 tonnes of sand are used to make the two pitches. The game is played on a touch-rugby basis, with each side allowed to take three tackles before the ball is turned over to the other side. Two halves of seven minutes each are played with five players on each side and rolling substitutions. With a large number of corporate teams competing, the tournament is now firmly established in the City of London sporting calendar and Ward hopes to expand the festival to other cities over the coming years.

## RUGBY NETBALL

The Rugby Netball League was established in 1907 and is played on Clapham Common in south London during the summer. As the name suggests, scoring involves dropping the ball into a net at either end of the pitch. Players can pass in any direction and there are no offside laws. The pace is frenetic and, with a sun-baked pitch, the tackles can be extremely hard.

*Time Out* described it as a 'bizarre hybrid of a sport', and, with its huge nets measuring around 1 m across and suspended 3.5 m in the air, Mike Bushell of BBC Sport called it 'netball for giants'.

# WHEELCHAIR RUGBY

Rugby also takes great pride in the diversity of its players and the wide range of abilities that flourish on the pitch. This Paralympic sport was created in 1976 by a group of Canadian wheelchair athletes. Originally called 'murderball' because of its aggressive, full-contact nature, the game was essentially a spiced-up version of wheelchair basketball.

Played on a hardwood court the same size as a basketball court, players score by carrying the ball over the goal line, but their opponents can use their wheelchairs to block and stop them. It is a fast-moving game, as players must pass or bounce the ball within ten seconds. More than 24 countries play the sport and it became a Paralympic sport in Sydney in 2000, with the USA taking home the first gold medal.

Mark Zupan, who captained the US team in 2004, said:

*❝ Breaking my neck was the best thing that ever happened to me. I have an Olympic medal. I've been to so many countries I would never have been, met so many people I would never have met. I've done more in the chair... than a whole hell of a lot of people who aren't in chairs. ❞*

# THE INTERNATIONAL TOURNAMENTS

..............................................................

For many, rugby is primarily a game of individual fixtures between sides with great rivalries going back generations. Traditionally, there has been less emphasis on the more formal leagues, cups and championships than in other sports. However, with professionalism and the growth of the game generally, the big international rugby tournaments have become increasingly important and popular. Here, then, are the many and various ways that international rugby players can get their hands on some silverware.

## THE SIX NATIONS

This tournament started life in 1882 as the Home Nations Championship contested by England, Scotland, Wales and Ireland. France joined in 1910 and suggested renaming the tournament the Five Nations. Italy joined in 2000 and then there were six.

In fact, there are a variety of trophies up for grabs – both real and imaginary – over the course of the tournament. Selected individual fixtures have their own trophies: the Calcutta Cup for the England v Scotland clash, the Centenary Quaich for the Scotland v Ireland fixture, and the Giuseppe Garibaldi Trophy for the France v Italy game. After that, there are trophies depending on how many games you win.

Teams play each other once only, alternating home and away over successive seasons. Two points are awarded for a win and one for a draw, and the side with the most points at the end wins the Championship Trophy, a sterling-silver cup first presented in 1993.

For England, Scotland, Wales and Ireland, there is an honour to be won called the Triple Crown, awarded to the side that beats all the other home nations in a season. There wasn't a trophy to accompany this award until 2006 when the sponsors RBS created a silver platter.

The most prestigious prize of all is a Grand Slam, which can be claimed by any side that wins all of its games in a given season. No physical trophy accompanies this one, but the team that achieves it gets bucketloads of kudos. The side that finishes bottom of the table is awarded the wooden spoon, although again no actual carved, cake-stirring implement is handed over.

# THE RUGBY CHAMPIONSHIP

This is the Southern Hemisphere's equivalent of the Six Nations, in which Australia, South Africa, New Zealand and Argentina compete. It was previously known as the Tri-Nations before Argentina joined in 2012. Inaugurated in 1996, the contest has been completely dominated by New Zealand, with the Kiwis winning 13 out of the first 20 competitions.

The teams play each other twice per season, home and away, and there are bonus points to encourage more tries and to provide an incentive for losing sides to keep their losing margin to seven points or fewer.

There are also individual fixture trophies within the tournament, including the Bledisloe Cup for the overall winner of the Australia v New Zealand games, the Freedom Cup for the victor of the fixtures between South Africa and New Zealand, the Mandela Challenge Plate for the winner of the Australia v South Africa games, and the Puma Trophy, which would leave something for Argentina to win if only they could beat Australia.

# THE RUGBY WORLD CUP

The Rugby World Cup is a relative newcomer to the international sporting calendar, but it already attracts the third-largest global audience for a sporting event. Although it was first mooted in the 1950s, it wasn't until the early 1980s that the Australian and New Zealand RFUs joined forces to put together a feasibility study.

On 21 March 1985 the committee of the International Rugby Board met in Paris to decide whether or not to go ahead with the idea. The home nations were opposed, fearing that it would inevitably become a huge commercial affair and undermine the game's amateur ideals. New Zealand, Australia and France were supportive, and when South Africa also declared in favour the vote was tied at 4–4. The committee debate went into extra time, first England and then Wales changed their minds, and the Rugby World Cup was born.

The first tournament was held in New Zealand and Australia in 1987. It was a 16-team invitational tournament and New Zealand won. The tournament has been held every four years since then but only really came alive in South Africa in 1995. Qualifying tournaments were introduced for the 1991 Rugby World Cup and they have helped to strengthen the game in the nations lower down the world rankings. By the time of the 2011 competition, 86 different nations took part in the early stages. The trophy stayed in the southern hemisphere for the first four competitions, perhaps explaining why those nations had been so keen on the idea. England secured the trophy for the first time with that drop goal from Jonny Wilkinson in the dying seconds of the final against Australia in Sydney in 2003.

When the World Cup tournament came to England in 2015, 2,477,805 fans cheered from the terraces as 2,439 points were scored. The final between New Zealand and Australia was enjoyed by an estimated audience of 120 million, although perhaps the Australians didn't enjoy watching it quite as much as everyone else.

# RUGBY LEAGUE WORLD CUP

Rugby league, having been a professional game for a lot longer, was a little quicker to get round to organising a world cup for its variant of the game. The first Rugby League World Cup was organised in France in 1954 with just four sides – Great Britain, France, New Zealand and Australia – playing in a league format, with the top two sides battling it out in a final. Great Britain won the first tournament and Australia won the next one three years later on their home soil. The tournament was then a little sporadic until the 1970s, when it began to be played on a home and away basis around the world. In 1995, to celebrate the centenary of the sport, it became a hosted tournament again, this time in England, with over 250,000 supporters attending the group stages and 66,000 watching Australia beat England in the final (Great Britain had by now split into separate teams representing the four home nations). By 2013 there were 14 teams competing, with Australia defeating New Zealand in the final. The tournament seems now to have settled on a four-year cycle.

# THE OLYMPICS

Rugby was a massive hit as it returned to the Olympics in Rio 2016, but its relationship with the global sporting festival goes back a lot further than that. The founder of the modern Olympics was the French educationalist Pierre de Coubertin, who in the 1880s toured the English public schools, including Rugby School, on his quest for academic inspiration. De Coubertin had read *Tom Brown's Schooldays*, the novel set in Rugby School with its graphic description of the game, and was inspired by the school's legendary headmaster Thomas Arnold, whom he saw as 'one of the founders of athletic chivalry'. De Coubertin felt that 'organised sport can create moral and social strength' and saw links to the Ancient Greek idea of the gymnasium, which artfully combined exercise, philosophical debate and nude bathing (coincidentally all the ingredients of a standard Saturday at any modern-day rugby club). De Coubertin was a huge fan of rugby and refereed the first ever French championship final in 1892 between Racing Club de France and Stade Français.

De Coubertin, having failed to convince the French educational authorities to adopt his rugby-inspired educational policies, set his sights instead on changing the whole world, proposing the re-establishment of the Olympic Games. Rugby featured in the games in Paris in 1900, London in 1908, Antwerp in 1920 and four years later again in Paris. The 1924 final was between the USA and France, but the Parisian crowd were so incensed when their side lost by 17 points to 3 that they invaded the pitch and beat several American supporters unconscious. So much for athletic chivalry!

Pierre de Coubertin stepped down as IOC President and rugby didn't make it back into the games for another 92 years. However, when it did, it came back with a new, seven-a-side format. Twelve nations were selected from global qualification competition in each of the men's and women's tournaments. Brazil, the host nation, was beset with economic challenges, so many of the stadiums (across all the sports) looked a little sparsely attended. Once the rugby sevens got going, however, the Deodoro Stadium where the rugby games were played was filled to 75–85 per cent capacity, attracting a crowd of 12,000 for the women's final between New Zealand and Australia. Before the games, many of those with an interest in the sport's continued global growth had hoped that the men's final would feature the USA, the reigning Olympic champions (albeit from 92 years earlier), who would bring with them a vast potential

TV audience. In the end the USA were knocked out in the group stage, but the emotional scenes when the tiny island state of Fiji won their first ever Olympic medal by beating Great Britain in the final will have captured the imagination of many new rugby fans around the world. Bill Beaumont, former England 15s captain and the current President of World Rugby, speaking after the tournament, said, 'Hopefully we have earned the right to be a permanent sport. We will be trying like mad to retain our status.' Rugby will feature again in the 2020 games in Tokyo and then will have to make its case for future inclusion.

## HONG KONG SEVENS

The Hong Kong Sevens has for many years been the premier international sevens competition, played in March every year, as 24 teams compete over three days for a prize fund of $150,000. The atmosphere in the South Stand of the Hong Kong Stadium can get very lively, with fancy dress, Mexican waves and the inevitable streakers. It is a hugely popular tournament with its fans, who will point out that if you ever get bored of the sevens, you can always turn round and watch the rugby.

## THE MEN'S WORLD RUGBY SEVENS SERIES

The Men's World Sevens series is the elite-level competition that has incorporated the Hong Kong Sevens since 1999. By the 2016/17 season the series had extended to ten legs, visiting

Dubai, Cape Town, Wellington, Sydney, Las Vegas, Vancouver, Hong Kong, Singapore and Paris before the finale in London.

The London Sevens finale fills up Twickenham Stadium for two days each May, with a colourful display of costumes and alcohol-fuelled antics in and around the games.

The series as a whole claims a total attendance of 715,000 fans, with 6,000 hours of action broadcast in over 100 territories.

## TOURNAMENTS FOR ALL

There are international tournaments that provide Test-level competition for the second-tier and emerging rugby nations. The Pacific Nations Cup began in 2005 and is the home for Test matches between Fiji, Samoa and Tonga. It has also in the past involved the Australian and New Zealand B teams, as well as Canada, Japan and the USA.

The Nations Cup features second- and third-tier sides, such as Portugal, Russia, Namibia, Georgia and Romania, and in some years development sides from the tier-one nations have also joined in.

From the start of the 2016 season European Rugby established a new-look Rugby Europe Championship to allow the next six top-ranked European sides (i.e. the six below the ones who compete in the Six Nations Cup) to compete in a league format. With leagues at four more levels below, as well as a promotion and relegation system, it should be possible over the coming years for a wider range of rugby-playing nations to rise up the rankings and increase the diversity and competitiveness of the international game.

# TROPHIES FOR ALL

It took just over a hundred years for the Rugby Football Union to sanction a formal competition between more than two club sides. Up until the early 1970s it had argued that leagues and knockout competitions were not in the best interests of the game.

However, in 1972 they launched an RFU cup competition for senior sides, bringing together a number of sides which had never previously played each other. That became the John Player Cup and through various sponsors has now morphed into the LV= Cup. Given the complex system of bonus points, play-offs and convoluted promotion and relegation regulations, those early administrators might have had a point. Let us look at the major trophies up for grabs at club level.

## AVIVA PREMIERSHIP
**(previously sponsored by Guinness, Zurich, Allied Dunbar and Courage)**

- League for the top 12 clubs in England.
- Teams play each other home and away.

- 4 points for a win, 2 points for a draw.

- 1 bonus point for losing a match by 7 points or fewer.

- 1 bonus point for scoring 4 or more tries in a game.

- The top four clubs qualify automatically for the European Rugby Champions Cup.

- The top four clubs also enter a set of finals. Teams 1 and 4 play in one semi-final and teams 2 and 3 play in another, the higher-placed side having home advantage.

- The winners play in a final at Twickenham, and the winner of that is then, and only then, crowned champions.

- The last-place club is relegated to the RFU Championship (formerly National Division One).

- Promotion from the Championship is subject to a set of minimum standards criteria, meaning that the club has to have a big enough ground and the appropriate facilities to cope with games in the top flight.

# THE SUPER LEAGUE

- The Super League is rugby league's premier club competition in Europe, with 12 sides competing, 11 from England and one from France.

- Most of the English clubs play in the game's heartlands of Yorkshire and Lancashire, conveniently connected by the M62.

- After the sides have all played each other home and away, the top eight sides go into a further round of games known as the Super 8s. After that the top four go into a set of play-offs in order to see who goes into the Grand Final.

- Since its foundation in 1996 the tournament has been dominated by rugby league's big four sides – Leeds, Bradford, Wigan and St Helens – with Hull and Warrington being the only other sides that have made it to a final.

## THE CHALLENGE CUP

- Rugby league's big knockout tournament, it has been running virtually uninterrupted since 1896, breaking only for two world wars. There are eight rounds of the tournament, with teams of different standards entering at different stages.

- Amateur teams compete in the first two rounds, and are joined by 14 League One teams for the third round. The Championship teams join in for the fourth round, followed by the bottom four clubs from the Super League, who join in for the fifth round. The big boys of the Super 8s come in for the sixth round.

- After semi-finals held at neutral venues, much of the north of England usually heads down to Wembley for the final.

- The original Fattorini Trophy, named after the Bradford silversmiths who created it in 1897, had to be recreated for the 2002 final as the original was wearing a little thin.

- Winners of the trophy have to follow a detailed code of practice setting out the conditions for its care. If it is outside a secure cabinet, it must be attended at all times, with someone sleeping in the same room as the trophy overnight. If it is driven anywhere, there have to be two people in the car. If it goes on a flight, it has to have its own seat.

## GUINNESS PRO12
**(originally known as the Celtic League and then the Magners League)**

- League for 12 sides from Wales, Ireland, Scotland, France and Italy.

- Points and bonuses are awarded along the same lines as the Aviva Premiership and the top four clubs go into a similar set of play-offs.

- The top-placed side in the league gets to choose the venue for the final.

## EUROPEAN RUGBY CHAMPIONS CUP
**(replaced the Heineken Cup from 2014)**

- Competition for 20 clubs, six from England and six from France. Wales, Scotland, Ireland and Italy between them get seven teams based on their performance in the Pro12. The final place is determined by a play-off between the sides that didn't quite make it in the other categories.

- Teams start in five pools of four, with a complex set of rules to mix up the nations and keep the top sides apart until the knockout stages.

- Pool winners and the three best-placed runners-up enter a knockout stage.

- The final is played at one of the Six Nations national stadiums.

# EUROPEAN RUGBY CHALLENGE CUP

- Competition for European clubs not in the European Rugby Champions Cup, plus two from a qualifying competition including Romanian and Georgian sides.

- 20 teams in five pools of four.

- The winners and the three best runners-up go into a set of quarter-finals and work their way towards a final.

- The winner then qualifies for the play-offs for the twentieth place in the European Rugby Champions Cup the following season.

With rugby's administrators being as they are, the rules for all the league and cup competitions described above will have been redrafted, debated and changed three or four times before I finish typing this paragraph, let alone get this book into your hands, but I'm sure the competitions themselves will continue to excite whatever the administrators get up to.

# HOW TO...

Rugby is a very warm and welcoming world, but there are a few things it would be helpful to know before dipping a tentative toe into the communal bath, as it were. There follow a few tips and suggestions for those of you who might be considering embarking on a rugby career, or for those of you who are wondering where yours might have gone wrong.

## HOW TO... JOIN A CLUB

These days joining a rugby club could not be simpler. With the aid of the internet most rugby union websites all around the world will have a mechanism whereby you can type in your address or postcode and somewhere in Silicon Valley a bunch of servers will whizz into action and within a few nanoseconds a list of nearby clubs will pop up on your screen. A couple of clicks later and you will have the contact details of a membership secretary, who again will probably have an online mechanism for helping you part with a modest social membership subscription.

Having said all that, it does have to be borne in mind that most rugby clubs are still run by older gentlemen who have spent the best years of their lives being battered around a rugby pitch or getting battered in a rugby club bar afterwards. Administrative and organisational tasks may occasionally stretch their few remaining synapses. The acquisition of IT skills may even have been overlooked by some of them, so it is probably not wise to rely solely on the internet, and you may even be able to uncover some hidden gems with a little more local research.

A quick read of your local papers may help to identify the right club for you to join. The back pages of most regional publications will, during the rugby season, have match reports from the leading clubs in your area. During the summer months, clubs that are actively looking for new members will try a variety of creative stunts to gain themselves a few column inches. My own club, Warlingham RFC, launched its own brand of condoms, decorated in club colours, in an attempt to gain some newspaper headlines and raise awareness among a certain key demographic.

Rugby clubs will accept you at any time of the year, but if you are keen to play, rather than just watch from the sidelines and drink in the bar, then tipping up during the pre-season training period will endear you to the coaches and selectors. Most clubs will endeavour to get players back together in July and August and many will organise touch rugby as an easy introduction to lure in new players. Often this will be on a weekday evening, giving people time to get home from work, changed and up to the training ground. Well-organised and sociable clubs might even manage to open the bar afterwards for a well-earned pint.

You don't have to play rugby to join a club, though. Most will welcome you with open arms if you turn up on a Saturday afternoon and support from the touchlines. A reduced social membership fee will allow you to use the bar, attend all the social events and generally absorb the atmosphere without having to get your boots dirty. However, at the end of the evening, after you have had a few drinks, beware the fourth XV captain, who will almost certainly try to persuade you to play at some point in the season.

## HOW TO... GET A GAME

For every side in every club there is a captain and for most of those skippers the job description includes recruiting and retaining players. In larger clubs, the first team may have a paid coach and a selection committee deliberating every week over who should be in the starting XV on Saturday, but for the lower sides such luxuries are rare. As a captain your every waking moment is spent trying to make sure you have enough players to get a side out at the weekend. Higher teams will want to poach players from your side. Higher authorities, like wives, husbands, girlfriends and boyfriends, will have competing attractions to lure away your star performers.

For these reasons it is always extremely easy to get a game in most rugby clubs. All you have to do is identify the captain of the lowliest side in your chosen club and make sure that he or she has your mobile phone number programmed into their phone. You might also have to make sure you are in the right WhatsApp or Facebook groups too, but if you are keen to play most clubs will somehow find you and find you a game.

It helps if you are not too fussy about what position you play in for your first few games. Offering to go in the front row, if you are of the right build and more or less know what to do there, will make you extremely popular with captains who have to supply an experienced front row and a few spares in order to ensure the game has properly contested scrums.

If all else fails and you find yourself unselected, the next best trick is to simply turn up an hour or so before kick-off with your boots and lurk. There are plenty of things that go wrong whenever anyone attempts to gather 15 rugby players into one place ready for a game. Rugby players are not always the brightest and the slightest navigational challenge – finding an away ground, for example – can leave many a captain desperately trying to rustle up extra players moments before the kick-off. The captain will be easy to spot. They will have a mobile phone stuck to their ear and will be frantically scribbling on a scrap of paper, trying somehow to work out how to spread such players as they do have around the pitch to make it look like they have 15. Simply wander up and offer your services and you will more than likely get a game.

## HOW TO... RUN A COMMUNAL BATH

Rugby is closely associated in many people's minds with a post-match communal bath. The image of a group of blokes sharing a deep hot bath, with a somewhat unsavoury cocktail of mud, sweat and playing-field turf coalescing into a floating, foaming scum, is enough to put many off the game altogether. In reality, communal baths have rather gone out of fashion, with most clubs preferring showers, which require a lot less water and are more hygienic. However, if you do come across a club with a proper bath it is well worth finding out how to fill it. There is actually nothing better after a cold, muddy and physically draining game of rugby than a decent soak in a deep hot bath with your fellow teammates and the opposition. As long as you can overcome any awkwardness about getting naked in front of a large group of people, you are away.

The key thing to remember about communal baths is that they take a long time to fill. You probably need to start filling it at half time or possibly even before the kick-off, depending on how fast the flow and how powerful the boiler is. You will need to put a few inches of cold water in first for safety and to keep the bath from scalding your teammates. If you are playing, try to find someone wearing a stripy blazer who has been around the club for a while and will appreciate the importance of getting the temperature, depth and timing just right. Get them to keep an eye on the bath while you play the second half of the game. Oh, and remember to put the plug in first.

**HOW TO...** DRINK A YARD

1. Don't!

2. If you must, start by handing over your car keys. You are not driving home today.

3. Remove as much clothing as you dare. There will be spillage, and your smart post-match shirt and club tie outfit will be ruined.

4. You may well be required to stand on a chair and, if so, make sure that there is plenty of headroom to lift up the yard glass high enough to empty it.

5. Take your time. Lawrence Hill of Bolton, Lancashire, is in the Guinness Book of Records for drinking a 2½ pint yard of ale in 6.5 seconds in 1964. You are not going to beat that, so don't try.

6. Twist the glass as you drink. It evens up the air pressure more gradually and should stop all the beer from tipping out at once.

7. If there is a big surge of beer, don't widen your mouth to try to catch it. It will all end up coming out of your nose, eyes and possibly even your ears – and that won't be pleasant for anyone, least of all you.

8. That's it really. You then just have to drink it.

9. Take a bow and congratulate yourself for keeping your rugby club entertained.

## HOW TO... PLAY DRINKING GAMES

It is one of life's happy coincidences that many of us who love rugby are also rather fond of the occasional alcoholic drink, enjoyed in moderation of course. Now, there are some enthusiastic proponents of both rugby and drinking who will be found in every rugby club bar waiting for the perfect opportunity to launch into some competitive drinking games. These are dangerous moments for the uninitiated. Launching into a newly initiated game after you have already had a drink or two, when you aren't entirely sure of the rules, and especially if you are vulnerable to peer pressure, can lead you down a very wobbly path and can end in a world of pain.

A rudimentary understanding of the basic principles of some of the more popular games set out on the following pages will help you to avoid some of the worst excesses and survive with your liver and dignity reasonably intact. It also helps if you start sober, and don't get drawn into any games if you have already had two or three pints. It won't end well if you do.

## BOAT RACE

Two teams line up on opposite sides of a long table, with their drinks in front of them. On the command 'Go!' the person at the head of each team downs their drink as quickly as possible and then places the empty glass upside down on their head. The next player then downs his drink and so on until each player has finished. The first team to all finish their drinks is the winner.

## 21s

This is a counting game with obscure rules that get harder to follow the drunker you become. Players sitting around a table call out a series of numbers in turn, starting with the number 1. Players then call out one, two or three consecutive numbers. If a player calls out a single number (e.g. 'two'), play continues in the same direction. If a player calls out two consecutive numbers (e.g. 'two, three'), the direction of play is reversed. If a player calls out three numbers, the next player is missed out.

Play continues until someone makes a mistake, which is pretty common even when you are sober, or calls out '21'. Players making a mistake, like playing out of turn, have to drink two fingers' worth of their drink. A player forced to say '21' has to down the remainder of their drink. Players gradually add new random rules and the game usually descends into a bewildering chaos of shouting, cheering and drinking.

## SPOOF

Each player has three coins. The players stand around in a circle and each one chooses to conceal one, two, three or none of the coins in their fist. Players then have to guess the total number of coins that are being concealed by all the players. No two guesses can be the same. If someone guesses correctly they are then safely out of the game. Other rounds follow and gradually more players drop out. The last person left in at the end is the loser and has to drink a forfeit.

## THE WIBBLY WOBBLY GAME

Tonbridge Juddians RFC claims to have introduced the Wibbly Wobbly game to Britain, where two teams line up so that the players can take it in turns to down a pint, run to a stump, place their head upon it and circle it ten times before setting off back to their teammates. Tonbridge eventually had to ban the indoor version after one month of playing it resulted in more injuries than the team could sustain.

## HOW TO... SING RUGBY SONGS

Rugby clubs have had something of a reputation for raucous communal singing. With alcohol lubricating the voice box and loosening the inhibitions, rugby songs have emerged as a musical genre all of their own.

However, in recent decades the tradition has perhaps declined a little. Some blame drink-driving laws for emptying clubhouses before anyone has had a chance to drink enough to enable them to channel their own interior operatic tenor. Alternatively, it could have more to do with the fact that people actually get a lot drunker a lot quicker nowadays and are nowhere near coherent enough to remember more than one line of any song.

However, with the advent of ubiquitous smartphones making it possible for even the drunkest prop to download lyrics and tunes from the comfort of the bar, there may be hope that the tradition can be gradually restored.

Most rugby songs depend heavily for their humour on the noble art of the double entendre, finding innocent phrases, perhaps drawn from the rugby game itself, to create a risqué suggestion whilst maintaining semi-plausible deniability and allowing the lyrics to be printed in a family publication. Here is one such example:

### 'If I were the marrying kind'

If I were the marrying kind,
Which thank the lord I'm not sir,
The kind of man that I would wed
Would be a rugby full-back.

And he'd find touch,
and I'd find touch,
We'd both find touch together.
We'd be alright in the middle of the night,
Finding touch together.

If I were the marrying kind,
Which thank the lord I'm not sir,
The kind of man that I would wed
Would be a wing three-quarter.

And he'd go hard,
and I'd go hard,
We'd both go hard together.
We'd be alright in the middle of the night,
Going hard together.

Centre three-quarter... pass it out
Fly half... whip it out
Scrum half... put it in
Hooker... strike hard
Prop forward... bind tight
Referee... blow hard

Do of course feel free to Google carefully – ideally whilst not at work – for further, less subtle verses. Whilst you're there, it is also worth choosing your own verse for one or two of the other popular rugby club songs. The charming ditty 'I used to work in Chicago' has opportunities for an endless variety of retail-based rudeness. Selecting one or two verses to memorise will enable you to join in when others are running out of inspiration.

Of course, it is also possible to engage the rugby club bar in a selection of entirely innocent, wholesome and uplifting songs suitable for a mixed and family audience. A particular favourite of mine is the delightful 'Sunshine Mountain', which if started when the mood is right, can have the entire club along with any guests and innocent bystanders up on chairs singing at the top of their lungs. The words and actions are as follows:

---

**'Sunshine Mountain'**

We're all going up Sunshine Mountain
(Standing on a chair, marching on the spot)
Where the gentle breezes blow
(Blow out through puffed cheeks three times)
We're all going up Sunshine Mountain
(marching on the spot)
Faces all a glow – o – o – oh
(Hands open at the side of your face, fingers apart like rays of sunlight)
Turn around
(Turn around, unsurprisingly)

---

**Put your hands up**
(Put your hands up – getting the hang of this yet?)
**Reach up to the sky**
(Yes, you guessed it – reach up to the sky)
**We're all going up Sunshine Mountain**
(A little bit more marching on the spot)
**You and I**
(Point to someone and encourage them to join you standing on a chair)
**You and I**
(Point at them again even more enthusiastically)
**You and I**
(Apply as much emotional pressure as you can muster until they relent and get up on a chair)

(Repeat until the entire clubhouse is up on a chair singing.)

## HOW TO... BECOME A TEAM CAPTAIN

It is a popular misconception that in a rugby club the captain is necessarily the best player in the team. This is not the case for most rugby sides. Professional teams and the first teams of larger clubs will typically pick their best player, or the one with the most leadership skills, as the captain on the pitch. Their role will be limited to a little motivational chat before and during the game and acting as the conduit for any conversations to be had with the referee. However, at the lower levels of the game the role of the captain is far wider, and most of the work required is off the pitch rather than on it.

So a second, third or fourth XV team captain does not need to be the strongest, fastest or most technically skilled person on the pitch. What they do need to be, however, is the most organised and reliable person off the pitch. Their job is to encourage, cajole and, if necessary, blackmail people to turn out and play for them, week after week. They need to have a well-organised contacts section in their mobile phone and know how to send group text messages and be a dab hand at communicating via email, WhatsApp, Facebook, Twitter, Instagram and possibly carrier pigeon.

As the task of captaincy for the lower sides is quite onerous and time-consuming, becoming a captain is relatively straightforward. Vacancies arrive every season as the incumbents tire of the phone calls and messages and worrying every week if they will have enough players for Saturday. As someone once said, 'Eighty per cent of success in life is from turning up.' Making an appearance at your club's Annual General Meeting and offering your services as captain for one of the lower sides is normally enough to clinch it. So keen are clubs to identify team captains that you probably only need to mention to one person in the bar that you are thinking about it and before you know it several committee members sporting stripy blazers will be surrounding you, offering drinks and other favours if you will agree to take on the role.

There are, of course, some advantages to being the captain:

- Your name is always first on the team sheet, as you are the one who is writing it out.

- You get to pick your favourite position, although, having said that, you may find that you will have to play in an unfamiliar role from time to time if you haven't managed to recruit players to fill all the slots.

- You get to chat to the referee during the game to discuss the finer points of interpretation of the laws, and if you disagree with his or her version you can fill in their little feedback form after the match and send it off to the referees' governing body.

- You get to decide the player of the day and award fines or forfeits for any misdemeanours.

- Occasionally you get to pick your opposition, as often during the week before a game fixtures get cancelled and rearranged as sides try to make sure they are up against the right level of opposition.

- In conjunction with your membership secretary you can get to decide who you will or will not play based on your experience from earlier matches or seasons.

- And, as a final treat, you get to create your version of history as you sit down on the Sunday afternoon to write the match report.

## HOW TO... WRITE A MATCH REPORT

One of the great traditions of the game of rugby is the preparation and publication of a well-crafted match report. A few paragraphs capturing the essential moments of the game and celebrating any particularly impressive performances can create a permanent record for all to see, which will help in the ever-present task of recruiting and retaining players. Everyone likes to have their efforts on a sporting field noticed, and in the lower leagues, with no television coverage or large crowds on the touchline to cheer every try, it is even more important to have a few words in a newsletter or on the club website that can be circulated and that your star players can show to their mum.

However, there are a few tips and potential pitfalls that you should be aware of before setting pen to paper or fingertips to keyboard:

1.   Check quickly after the game with the referee to be absolutely certain what the score was. Quite often in the confusion and exhaustion of a game you and your teammates may lose the ability to perform basic arithmetic. This problem can increase with every post-match pint that is consumed, so check the score early and write it down somewhere.

2.   Make sure you get the name of everyone who scored a try for your team. This might seem obvious but often it will be the odd mate of a mate who has turned up for the first time this week who scores. If they did score, you not only want to make sure they get a mention in the report, but you also need their phone number, email address, home address, Twitter handle, next of kin and dental records so that you can get hold of them again for future fixtures.

3. Check that everyone is OK to be mentioned in the match report. Sometimes you might have a player who has secretly made him or herself available for your team but really ought to be playing for another, more senior side. A quick agreement can usually be reached to allocate any points they might have scored to another regular member of the team or come up with a suitable pseudonym.

4. It is also worth remembering that some people's partners might not be entirely supportive of their decision to spend their Saturday afternoon playing rugby. They might prefer that they were helping out with some important domestic task such as putting up shelves or being sociable with some in-laws. They may have omitted to mention that they were planning to play rugby at all, allowing their partner to harbour the mistaken impression that they have just popped out for a pint of milk. You might be wise to leave them out of the match report altogether, along with anyone who was supposed to be at work.

5. Don't be too rude about the opposition. It is quite possible that they will read your match report in these days of instant communication and powerful search engines that trawl the internet. Over the years I have encountered too many players from other clubs who have returned in subsequent fixtures with a deep-seated grudge about something I might have said in a match report of our previous encounter, a grudge that can only be settled with a hard shoulder into my ribs.

6.  Keep it short and sweet. You don't need to describe every single pass, tackle, scrum and maul. Pick out the key stories of the day, the memorable moments and the best bits of banter, and build your match report around that. A quick list of names and points scorers at the end should ensure you have covered all the basics.

7.  Thank all the players and particularly those who have turned up for the first time, but beware... don't be too effusive about any new stars who have played outstandingly. A glowing mention in the match report might mean that other more senior sides in your club come sniffing around and try to tempt them away to their side. If they have played well, let them know that you will be paying them the highest possible compliment of leaving them entirely out of the match report so that they don't get pinched and can carry on scoring tries for your lowly side against your lowly opposition for the rest of the season.

## HOW TO... BECOME ONE OF THE 57 OLD FARTS

As we noted earlier, it was Will Carling as England captain who christened the game's administrators in England with such flatulatory flourish. It is a title that they now wear with pride as they continue to run the game. Every nation has a similar structure as the not-so-great and the not-so-good find their way of rising to positions of power within our beloved sport. Another former England captain Martin Johnson put it well when he said in his autobiography:

HOW TO...

*" A lot of people mistakenly think that major rugby
matches are put on for guys to play and for people to come
and watch. That is not the case. They are actually organised
for the benefit of people in blazers. "*

So, whilst we might bemoan the way that the game is run from
time to time, it turns out that, within England at least, there is a
process whereby anyone with a little patience and determination
could, in theory, find themselves on the controlling committees
and walking the corridors of power at rugby's headquarters in
Twickenham. Here are the steps you need to follow if you want
to end up an old fart:

1. Get elected to the club committee – most clubs are always
   looking for someone to serve as social secretary or in a
   promotional role.

2. Bide your time until the chair steps down – most people
   only manage two or three years in that sort of role, as the
   infighting and power politics in even the smallest, friendliest
   club can become irksome after a while.

3. Get yourself elected as club chairperson. Once there is a
   vacancy, so long as you are reasonably agreeable and can
   control a committee meeting, you will find that there won't
   be a huge amount of competition for the role as chair.

4. As chair, you will then be able to find a county level
   committee to sit on where you can busy yourself
   administering local leagues and disciplinary committees.

5. Before you know it there will be a vacancy for chair of your county union and, if you have managed to be affable and clubbable enough with your fellow county committee members, you might just be the Buggins who gets to have your turn.

6. Lo and behold, you are now entitled to a seat on the game's governing body and all that follows from there.

Now, this system may not be the best process for getting the right people in place to run a huge national professional game. In fact, it probably isn't. There have been tweaks and adjustments to the process over the years, with places being allocated on the governing body for women, schools, referees, players and so on. But the basic system remains: club blazers are traded up for county blazers and then national blazers in turn. To change it, one would need to use the same system to get to the top, so getting on your local club committee could be the first step to glory and changing the game for the better. To paraphrase the Irish political theorist and philosopher Edmund Burke, the only thing necessary for the triumph of old fartery is for good men to do nothing. For the love of rugby, what is stopping you?

**HOW TO...** GO ON TOUR

One of the delights of the game today is how well it lends itself to a tour, when a side packs its bags, kisses its loved ones goodbye and settles in for an extended trip filled with rugby, good humour and beer. As English Victorian gentlemen travelled and settled around the world, taking the game with them, very soon overseas tours became a possibility.

In 1888 the first Lions tour took place, essentially as a ruse to get some cricket promoters out of a spot of financial bother. Two separate teams of English cricketers had been touring Australia in 1887–88 and had nearly bankrupted the organisers in the process. Rather than give up, go home and face their creditors, they hatched a plan to put together a rugby tour, given they had already invested quite a lot of money in getting Down Under and establishing contacts with the different sports clubs and municipal authorities. They also managed to persuade some of the cricketers to stay on and play some rugby before going home.

Twenty-two additional players were recruited in England, mostly from northern English clubs plus a handful from Wales and Scotland. After sailing for six weeks on a boat from Gravesend they met up with the tour organisers in Port Chalmers and began a series of 35 games in New Zealand and Australia – of which they lost only two. They even tried their hand at a spot of Aussie rules football, winning seven games and drawing in three.

The Lions' penchant for hard drinking clearly began with this tour. According to Charlie Mathers, who kept a diary of the tour, the two Scottish tourists, Dr John Smith and Dr Herbert Brooks, both played rugby while intoxicated. Brooks reported more euphemistically that throughout the tour the team had received a 'hearty' reception wherever they went.

Tragically, halfway through the tour they lost their captain Robert Seddon who was killed in a boating accident on the

FOR THE LOVE OF RUGBY

Hunter River in West Maitland, New South Wales. He was buried in West Maitland in his flannel trousers and rugby top in the Campbells Hill Cemetery, after a procession led by 180 local players and the mayor and aldermen of the town.

When the tourists returned to England on 11 November after eight months abroad, the different nations had all learnt new things about the game from each other, and the Lions had established a relationship with rugby fans in the southern hemisphere that would see the tours continue throughout the following century and no doubt through the current one, too.

You won't need to book an eight-month sabbatical to go on a rugby tour these days, but you will need to start planning quite some way in advance. The secret of a successful tour is all in the planning and preparation and getting organised well in advance. There are companies who specialise in organising rugby tours and will arrange flights, accommodation, opposition and other extracurricular activities for a modest management fee. However, you can with a little effort put one together yourself, so here is your handy checklist for everything you might need for a triumphant rugby tour:

1.  Select your opposition carefully. If you are travelling abroad there can be a huge risk of ending up playing an entirely inappropriate opposition. The amateur side Dorchester Gladiators found this out the hard way on their Easter tour to Romania in 2000. A well-meaning embassy official took it upon himself to arrange a rugby fixture, but a misunderstanding somewhere along the line led to the national stadium being booked and a side packed with international players lining up

against the British amateurs. Not only that, but the game was all set to be broadcast live on national television and played in front of a huge crowd. Whilst the Romanians were warming up on the pitch, the terrified Dorchester side were nursing hangovers and nervously smoking cigarettes. Only once the game started did the Romanians realise the mismatch and, after scoring a succession of points, they eased off the hapless visitors. The final score was 60–17 to the hosts.

2.  Keep the travel and accommodation as simple and as cheap as possible. The more you can keep the costs down, the more people will be able to come along with you and the better your tour will be. Try to keep everyone travelling together and all staying in one place if at all possible. One Warlingham Rugby Club tour to Paris split over two hotels caused a few problems as one of the players returned to the wrong hotel having bailed out early during an evening's heavy drinking. When he found his room key wouldn't work he somehow persuaded the hotel's night porter to give him a replacement key to the room of someone else on the tour. The rightful owner returned to his room to find the wrong person in his bed, so headed off to find another room and another bed. This set off a chain of events that ended up with half the touring party in the wrong rooms and all feeling very confused the following morning.

3.  Everything takes a little longer than you might have hoped, so plan in plenty of time. The simple act of getting 20 rugby players from your hotel and into taxis can take ages, especially if you have to go past any bars to get to the taxi rank.

4.  International drinking rules are usually applied to tours. Those can include enforced left-handed drinking, replacing your glass on the table with a double tap, and making sure that drinks are always a thumb's distance from the edge of the table. Infringements result in the offender having to see off a set quantity of their drink – one or two fingers' depth or even the whole glass for major offences.

5.  Fancy-dress costumes make for a good atmosphere and are helpful when trying to herd the group. If everyone in your group is sporting a DayGlo morphsuit they are a lot easier to spot in a crowded bar. At the very least some matching tour stash should be organised. People will usually stump up for a tour T-shirt or playing top and, if you can buy them in large enough numbers, the price can be reasonable.

6.  It used to be the rule that 'What goes on tour, stays on tour', but in these modern days of smartphones and cheaper international internet access, what goes on tour usually goes on Facebook – so don't do anything you wouldn't be happy for your family and friends and work colleagues back home to see.

## HOW TO... UNDERSTAND THE LAWS

*❝ Rugby is a wonderful show: dance, opera and, suddenly, the blood of a killing. ❞*
**RICHARD BURTON, WELSH ACTOR**

Rugby is at its heart a fairly simple game, but the opportunities to gain strategic advantage through intelligent gameplay are practically endless. There is also a delicate interplay between the tactics employed by the skilled player and the development of the laws of the game. While coaches and captains will conspire to contrive new ways of winning, the laws of the game are tweaked and twiddled almost every year to refine the sporting spectacle and keep people relatively safe.

As we have already seen, rugby has laws drawn up by lawyers, as opposed to rules made up by rulers or other items found in school geometry sets. The laws are designed to encourage a physical battle to see which players can carry the ball furthest and fastest, and which players are strong enough to stop them. The guiding principles in the opening chapters of the International Rugby Board law book set out how they attempt to balance the contradictions that arise from encouraging players in 'exerting extreme physical pressure' while at the same time making sure not to allow anyone to 'wilfully or maliciously inflict injury'.

All the laws seek to reward superior skill. So if one side kicks the ball out of play because they cannot see a way through to run it up the pitch, the opposing side gets the advantage of the throw-in at the lineout. If a player can't catch a pass and knocks the ball forwards, the opposing side gets the advantage of their scrum half getting to put the ball into the middle of the scrum (the put-in).

The law about passing the ball backwards is a primary example of that principle in action. If for any reason a player doesn't feel brave enough or strong enough to carry the ball forwards and has to pass it, they have to pass it backwards. If you are not going to run forwards with the ball, you certainly can't move it forwards by flinging it up the field. You can save that sort of behaviour for netball.

The game, your fellow players, the supporters on the touchline, even William Webb Ellis watching from somewhere up above, are all willing you to run with the ball as hard as you can, only stopping to pass it to one of your teammates when there really is no alternative.

## KEEPING IT INTERESTING

There is one special law that when called upon can override all other laws in the interests of keeping the game entertaining. It's called the 'advantage law' and it means that referees can acknowledge but wilfully ignore any transgressions while waiting to see if the transgressed side can gain some sort of advantage without any help from the officials.

As the novelist and rugby union referee Derek Robinson said,

*The advantage law is the best law in rugby, because it lets you ignore all the others for the good of the game.*

Once again the principle of 'fine disregard' is applied to increase the joy that is obtained from the opportunity to play the game.

## HOW TO... WIN MORE GAMES

Rugby is of course more than just a battle of brute force. Obviously physical strength is important but an ability to make clever decisions can be just as influential in determining the outcome of any given game. A combination of a commanding physical presence, a degree of bravery and an ability to spot tactical opportunities in a fast-moving game makes for a great player. Two or three people like that on your side can make for a great game. Here are some pointers to help you develop the combination of skills you need in your team:

# TACTICS FOR FORWARDS

## SCRUMS

To the outside observer the scrum might not seem like a very tactical part of the game – a heap of players pack down together, the ball is popped into the middle and, after much huffing and puffing, the ball seems to pop out again somewhere else. The reality, as all forwards will tell you, is very different. Grouped under the heading of 'dark arts' are a number of micro-strategies available to the more advanced player.

With such great forces at work, a small adjustment in body position can make a huge difference in a scrum. When a front row is struggling, often the best response is for the props to try to be fractionally lower as the two packs engage. A lower body position enables the props to push up at a slightly different angle and gives their pack a marginal advantage.

A well-organised pack may also try to slightly wheel the scrum round, without the referee noticing, so that the whole team are in a better position when the ball comes out and the opposition's defenders are blocked from getting to it.

If things are going well in the scrum and you are not being pushed backwards there is also a tactical decision to make about how long to keep the ball in the scrum at the feet of the number 8. You might want to keep the ball in the scrum and push forwards a few yards, just to edge up the pitch a little, sapping the strength of your opposing pack. If things are not going so well, however, you want to get the ball out quickly, give it to the backs, and let them try to kick or run their way out of trouble.

## LINEOUTS

Lineouts are also packed with tactical choices. Each team will have its own set of codes to communicate where the hooker is going to try to throw the ball and what the catcher should do with the ball when they get it. A lineout throw that goes close to the front may increase the chances of a safe secure catch, keeping possession and allowing the pack to make a little progress. Alternatively, if your hooker has a good accurate throwing arm, getting the ball to the back of the lineout, and more quickly across the park, will stretch out the opposition's defences and may give you more chances to score. There is a choice about whether to catch the ball and have all the forwards huddle round into an attacking maul to drive up the pitch, or quickly flick the ball to the scrum half while still being held up in the air, 'off the top', enabling the backs to have a run.

The entire tactics of front-row play can be summed up in the following infographic, which has been drawn up in collaboration with some of the world's finest rugby strategists and sports scientists.

## KEEPING THINGS SIMPLE (FOR THE BENEFIT OF FORWARDS)

Are the opposition forwards bigger and stronger than yours?

**YES**

**NO**

Get the ball as quickly as possible to the backs and let them try to run around them.

Keep the ball in the forwards and drive up the pitch as far as you can.

# ATTACKING MOVES FOR BACKS

The job of the backs is essentially to find gaps in the opposition defences and run through them carrying the ball. Their strategy and tactics are geared towards creating more of those gaps and getting their players into the right place at the right time to exploit them.

The tricks and techniques used in the forwards may be known as the 'dark arts', but for deception and deviousness you should look no further than the sorts of things the backs get up to as they seek a small advantage over their opposition. Backs' moves are filled with dummy passes and runners coming out of surprising positions at unusual angles. There are lots of histrionics, as centres, wingers and full backs attempt to trick the defenders into going in one direction as they set off in another. The side that is better at playing the theatrics and the mind games is more likely to get a breakthrough and a try-scoring opportunity.

## A SIMPLE BACKS' MOVE

In this move the full back joins the line of attackers, giving them an extra person. As the ball gets to the outside centre the winger moves in closer to the centre, drawing in the opposition player marking him. The ball is then passed straight to the full back, who catches the ball while running at speed through the gap that has been created between the last defender and the touchline.

## A MORE COMPLICATED BACKS' MOVE

Here the ball is passed to the inside centre (number 12), who then turns around with his back to the opposition and shapes as if to make one of two dramatic dummy passes. The first is to the fly half who is running around apparently to catch a loop pass. The second is made in the direction of the outside centre (number 13), who is running through in the opposite direction. By this point the opposition defenders should have moved to where the dummy runners were heading and, with a bit of luck, left a gap for the blind-side winger who has run over from the other side of the pitch to exploit it.

There is, of course, plenty that can go wrong with any backs' move. Players have to time their runs absolutely perfectly so that when and if they do catch the ball they are in the right place and running at full speed. Dummy runs need to look convincing – and are often accompanied by a large shout calling for the ball – but not so convincing that they confuse the player making the pass. Most importantly, everyone needs to remember the calls and codes and not make it completely obvious to the defenders what they are about to do.

Sadly, however, the lot of the back in rugby is not always a happy one. On a cold, windy and wet afternoon, in the middle of winter, it is quite common for long periods of the game to pass without the ball finding its way to the backs at all. The most frustrating thing as a backs player can be to spend the hour before the game rehearsing and perfecting a series of wonderful elaborate moves, only to find that once the game starts the forwards either refuse to give you the ball or, even worse, keep losing it to the opposition.

# DEFENSIVE STRATEGIES FOR BACKS

In defence there are tactical choices to be made. At its simplest, it often boils down to a choice between a 'drift' or a 'blitz' defence.

## DRIFT DEFENCE

In a drift defence, the backs will try to shepherd the attacking side towards the touchline by pushing forwards on the inside shoulder of each attacking player and allowing the defensive line to be slightly sloped with the outside players hanging back. In a set-piece play from a scrum, it requires a little assistance from one of the flankers to put pressure on the attacking fly half, and that allows the defending side to drift across and gives them one extra defensive player.

## BLITZ DEFENCE

The blitz defence is a much more aggressive approach, as the name implies. The defending line rushes forwards as a straight line, putting pressure on all the attackers and often forcing them to make mistakes. It cuts down the time the attackers have to make decisions but at the same time it also commits defenders – which is fine if they are the sort of defenders who never miss a tackle, but it makes them vulnerable to an attacking side with a few moves of its own.

## GAME PLAN

Occasionally the forwards and the backs will agree a 'game plan', a broad agreement about how long the forwards will try to hang on to the ball before passing it out to the backs. Players will talk about one, two or three phases of attack where the forwards take the ball until they are stopped. Only then will the backs be given the ball and invited to run around. Game plans, however, very often go out of the window once the referee blows the whistle to start the game. Many a terrified forward will completely forget the strategy in the face of a ferocious onslaught from the opposition.

At different stages of the game you might see the forwards repeatedly picking up the ball from the back of a ruck, that wonderful name for a seemingly random heap of players piled on top of the ball, and running just a few feet into the next tackle. This can go on for some time as the attacking side attempts to draw in all the defending side's forwards, wearing them out, and perhaps forcing them to make a mistake and concede a penalty. Then, when the scrum half thinks the time has come and enough damage has been done, he or she will pass the ball out to the backs to exploit any space that has now been created.

## HOW TO... TURN PROFESSIONAL

So your darling child is showing a little promise at rugby and you are wondering, just wondering, whether he or she might make it as a professional player. Is this a career path that you should gently guide them down? You might fancy a professional career for yourself after a season or two outshining your teammates at your local club, and you might be thinking about your options. Well, the odds are not great and the rewards are modest, but there is now at least, certainly in England, a system for bringing on the best of our young rugby talent and preparing people for a successful professional career.

Most professionals learn the game at school or in local rugby clubs, and the best find their way into junior county sides. From there about a thousand 14–18-year-olds in England are recruited into Elite Player Development Groups for weekly coaching, conditioning and fitness. Teenagers, of course, develop at odd intervals and in inconvenient ways, so it takes a few years for talent to emerge into the next stage. Regional academies exist at all the Aviva Premiership sides and a couple of the Championship clubs, and around four players a year are offered academy contracts at the age of 18 for each of those clubs. The salaries are not high at this stage, being somewhere in the region of £10,000 per year, barely enough to keep any self-respecting teenager in hoodies and Haribo. They will stay in the academies for two to four years, with potential front-row forwards taking a little longer to mature, and then roughly 75 per cent are offered places in their senior squad.

> *" As players dream of a future in professional rugby and even playing for England, this ambition must be tempered with the knowledge that only the very talented will achieve the levels to make a sustained career from the game. "*
> **STUART LANCASTER, FORMER ENGLAND COACH**

First-team players from the English public schools will inevitably have a head start when it comes to grabbing a professional career, and many of those schools will offer generous scholarships to promising players. The academy system is helping kids from more modest backgrounds to make it onto the international stage. England prop Alex Corbisiero made it into the Surrey under 17s and then into the London Irish academy without going to an expensive rugby-playing private school. England second-row Courtney Lawes went from a school side into Northampton Old Scouts, a feeder club for the Premiership side Northampton Saints, and from there into the academy and a glittering international career.

There are a total of 600 players in the Aviva Premiership in England and on average they expect their playing careers to last until they are 33. Average salaries are in the region of £85,000 per year although the star players with international contracts can earn considerably more. As a result of injuries and the pressure to stay fit, 18 per cent of all Premiership players end each season without a contract for the next one. Some may go abroad, but many will either drop down to the Championship, where salaries are closer to £25,000, or out of the game altogether.

In the lower leagues some players are semi-professional, getting paid by the match to supplement their income from a separate career. As you head down the leagues, tensions sometimes arise between clubs that can afford to pay their players and clubs that either choose or are forced to remain strictly amateur. A sudden injection of cash from a wealthy backer can see new players recruited and a season or two of great results and promotions until the money runs out and the club slides back down the leagues again.

At whatever level you play, you will of course still do it for the love of rugby. Even with a salary and the prospect of fame and international stardom, no one can play rugby successfully without a little passion for the game. It is, I imagine, quite nice to get paid for playing the game. It is equally nice, however, to part with a club membership subscription and the occasional match fee to play the game just for the love of it.

# CALL TO ARMS

● ● ● ● ● ● ● ● ● ● ● ● ● ● ● ● ● ● ● ● ● ● ● ● ● ● ● ● ● ● ● ● ● ● ● ● ● ● ● ●

**❝** *The women and men who play on that rugby field are more alive than too many of us will ever be. The foolish emptiness we think we perceive in their existence is only our own.* **❞**

**VICTOR CAHN, AMERICAN WRITER**

Every year, rugby puts on a great display of international sportsmanship. With phenomenal games played by magnificent athletes in packed stadiums, rugby gives some of the best sporting entertainment in the world.

The benefits to wider society are huge. With over a hundred nations now playing the game, its power to strengthen international friendships is well recognised. As more and more people discover its joys every year, rugby is set to continue to go from strength to strength.

It is a simple game that can be appreciated from the safety of the sofa or the stands without any need for a huge degree of technical understanding. With a little more knowledge it can become a richer experience, and those who take up the opportunity to play it gain an even greater enjoyment of the strategies and tactics employed by the best sides.

In some cases, rugby has grown to become more than just a sport. Where there is a rugby club there are people who come together to play a game but often end up forming a community. The people who support each other physically on the pitch are the same people who support each other socially, emotionally and occasionally commercially off the pitch. The extended rugby family is a strong one and it sticks together.

For rugby to continue to grow and spread more joy around the world it needs players, supporters and volunteers. If you are a parent then you might want to think about dropping your little darlings off at a nearby rugby club on a Sunday morning, assuming of course that they run a mini or junior rugby section. This has the added advantage of giving you an hour or so uninterrupted with the Sunday papers. You might even find a degree of enjoyment supporting them from the touchline. If you get really keen, well, the world is your oyster. Rugby will always welcome those who are willing to pull on some boots, pick up a tackle bag and allow themselves to be run at and occasionally knocked over by small boys and girls carrying a rugby ball.

If you are already involved with a rugby club and worrying about a shortage of volunteers, don't worry: help is already at hand. A report by rugby sponsors Zurich found that 51 per cent of English former players would volunteer at their local rugby club if only someone had asked them. Rugby retains a loyal family of support ready to pick up a tackle bag and coach and support the next generation of players.

Rugby clubs have grown over the years as people have made time for the simple but necessary little bits of organisation to keep them ticking over: filling in forms, sending off emails, remembering to bring a first-aid kit. Rugby clubs have thrived when one or two enthusiastic types have gone to the trouble of creating a team from scratch and setting up a few more fixtures.

So the next time you are making a New Year's resolution to lose some weight, get fit or just get out more, why not point your newfound motivation and drive towards your nearest local rugby club. The Olympic movement has shown how powerful volunteering can be at multiplying the enjoyment as well as the economic and social legacy from major sporting events. Rugby, too, will benefit in the future if it taps into that spirit.

Rugby is a game to be played as well as watched and there are plenty of team captains and coaches all around the world looking for an extra player or two to make sure that they have a full side to play on Saturday. It will be easy to come up with one or two reasons why you shouldn't play: lack of fitness, lack of ability, lack of time or lack of boots. But there are many more reasons why you should play.

So, for the love of rugby, here is just a selection of the many reasons why you should not only continue to enjoy following and watching this fine sport, but why you should find a pair of boots and, if at all possible, keep playing until the great referee upstairs blows the final whistle.

## WE LOVE RUGBY BECAUSE...

1. Rugby is a far better way of keeping fit and is much cheaper than going to the gym. Other people talk to you and you have to keep working out until the referee blows the final whistle.

2. People who play team sports are actually, and this has been scientifically proven, happier than other people.

3. In rugby this might be something to do with the pre- and post-match huddle. When else can you get a hug from 15 people all at the same time?

4. Rugby is far better than football in that no one wastes time arguing with referees or writhing around on the floor in fake agony whenever another player gets anywhere near them.

5. Rugby supporters can generally be trusted to drink before, during and after a game without necessarily causing a major riot.

6. Rugby is a total body workout combining cardiovascular effort running around in the backs and muscle-building strength work in the forwards.

7. Rugby players have been sharing the joys of a hot tub since well before they became a feature of expensive spas and health retreats.

8. Mud is extremely good for your complexion.

9. Rugby gives you the perfect excuse to enjoy the sinus-clearing, skin-tingling benefits of Deep Heat, Tiger Balm or Ralgex.

10. Being a member of a rugby club gets you into a ballot for tickets for the internationals.

11. Half-time oranges are delicious.

12. So are half-time glasses of port.

13. Playing in the scrum means you have slightly more idea of what is going on when watching it being done professionally.

14. Playing in the front row of the scrum often means that your facial features can be used to frighten and discipline small children.

15. Cauliflower ears can be counted as one of your five a day.

16. You have an excuse for a romantic trip to Paris or Rome once every other year during the Six Nations.

17. You can enjoy a spot of communal singing without having to listen to a long sermon in church first.

18. Play rugby over a few years and you will inevitably pick up quite a lot of 'stash', and the rugby shirt is a style classic that never goes out of fashion.

19. You can enter a boat race (post-match drinking game) without having to go to Oxford or Cambridge.

20. If you drop a pass or fail to pick up a bouncing ball you can always blame the odd shape rather than your own incompetence.

21. Playing rugby will give you a group of friends for life.

22. No matter what shape or size you are, there will always be a place for you somewhere in a rugby team.

23. If none of those reasons appeal, you could always become a referee.

# THE FUTURE OF THE GAME

.........................................................

Rugby is heading towards its 200th birthday and is looking in remarkably fine fettle. The game continues to attract new players and new audiences and every year a few more nationalities join the global rugby family. As every generation picks up the ball and runs with it, the world seems to get a little more oval-shaped.

As this little book heads towards the final whistle, it is time to take out the crystal ball and see what we think might happen next to rugby. The first step is to consider which of the trends from the past are set to continue into the future and on that front the most significant change that has happened to rugby was probably when rugby union joined rugby league in becoming professional. The impact of that decision is still being felt and continues to be played out. Money doesn't grow on trees and professional player salaries have to be paid somehow. Inevitably it is the millions of supporters of the game who, for the love of rugby, will find themselves financing the professional game, either through buying tickets to games or through buying the products advertised in the TV breaks or on sponsorship boards around the pitch.

Rugby by its very nature will always attract competitive types and, just as rugby players compete on the pitch, rugby club owners will inevitably compete off the pitch. That means competing for those supporter numbers and their share of the TV audience. The more money and time that rugby fans put into the professional game, the less money and time might be put into the community level game. That could be a worry for those of us who enjoy playing the game as well as watching it.

Anecdotally, there are things that would suggest a link between the growth of the professional game and difficulties in the community game. When the game first went professional many clubs found themselves losing players almost overnight and have ended up putting out fewer sides at the weekend as a result. During the 2015 Rugby World Cup in England it definitely seemed harder to wrestle players away from the terraces or their TV sets and, as the tournament came at the start of the season, fewer people seemed to get into the habit of playing, with the lower leagues suffering cancelled games as a result. There is also a recent trend for the English Premiership sides to put on so-called 'big games', where once or twice a season they book Twickenham or Wembley, have a massive marketing push and bring in thousands of extra supporters to pack out a stadium. That makes for a great atmosphere in the stadium, but it does sometimes make it difficult for a fourth XV captain to find enough players to get a side out.

There is another way of looking at this, of course. In order to keep growing, the professional game will need to put on an ever more impressive show in order to bring in the crowds. The huge marketing push needed to fill bigger stadiums will not just be appealing to those who already play the game; it will be bringing new fans into the rugby family. As the players themselves become bigger stars and the sporting stories capture the imagination of a wider audience, it is easy to see more and more people finding a love for rugby and more and more new converts to the game pulling on a pair of boots and taking to the rugby pitch.

Whatever happens in reality, the reassuring thing to know is that those in charge of the professional game are also people who will have the interests of the community game at heart, too. Pretty much everyone on any committee of influence in rugby will be there because they have experienced at some point the joy of running with a rugby ball purely for fun, rather than to pay the mortgage. They do what they do for the love of rugby and so one can hope that the numbers of people watching the game and the numbers playing, both professionally and purely for pleasure, will all keep increasing.

The other long-term trend in the sport has been for the game to become that little bit safer. Every year sees a little rule change here and there to try to lower the risk of players being seriously hurt. Scrums in particular now feel like less dangerous places to be as a result of changes over the last few years. Asking props to pre-bind before engaging has reduced the terrifying impact of bringing two huge packs together, with the members of the front row literally putting their necks on the line. As a result it ought to be easier to recruit players to the front row, giving more people the pleasure of learning the so-called dark arts.

Some will, of course, argue that health and safety changes destroy the essential nature of the game as a real test of physical strength and character, but no one really wants to see their teammates and fellow players of the game permanently disabled as a result of playing a ball game. Sensibly bringing young people into the game with the risks carefully managed has to be the right approach, too. Young children in England start with tag rugby, where rather than tackling each other, they compete to rip a tag from their opponents, which is attached to a belt with Velcro. This gives them the chance to enjoy the thrill of the game without terrifying their parents on the touchline. A game that gets steadily safer, without losing its essential charm, has to have an encouraging future.

Another healthy sign is the trend for rugby to become a more diverse sport. Steadily increasing the numbers of women playing the game and making sure that the sport is accessible to people from all social backgrounds will help the game to develop and strengthen. Rugby's triumphant return to the Olympic stage will no doubt expand the game's appeal, and the shorter form of the sevens game will win over new audiences and recruit more players from all walks of life.

Rugby has clearly changed over its first couple of centuries, so it is reasonable to assume that it will continue to evolve over the next few. As it responds to social change and external pressures, there is no doubt that the game will find new ways to entertain and amuse us. One thing is for certain. Those of us who love it will continue to evangelise and enthuse about the game that brings us all so much pleasure and joy. We will keep encouraging ever more people to join a club and, for the love of rugby, discover and share in our wonderful oval ball game.

# RUGBY PUB QUIZ

∙∙∙∙∙∙∙∙∙∙∙∙∙∙∙∙∙∙∙∙∙∙∙∙∙∙∙∙∙∙∙∙∙∙∙∙∙∙∙∙∙∙∙∙

## QUESTIONS

### ROUND 1: GLOBAL RUGBY KNOWLEDGE

1. 'Subdue and Penetrate' is the motto of which international side?

2. Name the Irish playwright, novelist and poet who coined the phrase 'My drinking team has a rugby problem'.

3. Which Hollywood star played the South African captain Francois Pienaar in the film *Invictus* about the 1995 World Cup?

4. Following an upgrade at Murrayfield, and a Scotland-wide competition, what was donated to Caithness Rugby Club by the Scottish RFU in 2013?

5. Which side waited 8,741 days between their first and second ever Rugby World Cup victories, the latter coming at Brighton Community Stadium on 19 September 2015?

6. What was Welsh International Gareth Thomas the first professional rugby union player to do openly in December 2009?

7. Name the Australian scrum half who was capped 139 times for his country between 1994 and 2007.

8. Prior to becoming England captain in 2016, what did hooker Dylan Hartley spend 54 weeks of his rugby career doing?

9. Which side came fourth in the 2015 Rugby World Cup?

10. Which nation used the same 15 players throughout the entire length of its Five Nations Grand Slam-winning campaign of 1977?

## ROUND 2: STADIUMS
Name the English Premiership teams that play at the following stadiums:

1. Recreation Ground

2. Sandy Park

3. Kingsholm Stadium

4. The Stoop

5. Headingley Carnegie Stadium

6. Welford Road

7. Kingston Park

8. Franklin's Gardens

9.  AJ Bell Stadium

10. Allianz Park

## ROUND 3: TOP 5 STADIUM CAPACITIES

Name the top 5 stadiums in the world where rugby is played in order of capacity, with the largest first. Award 1 point for each correctly identified stadium and 1 point for placing it in the right position.

## ROUND 4: NICKNAMES

Name the players associated with the following nicknames:

1.  36

2.  Shaggy

3.  Chariots

4.  Pitbull

5.  Billy Whizz

6.  The Fun Bus

7.  Uncle Fester

8.  Billy Bumface

9.  The Honey Badger

10. Judith

## ROUND 5: WIPEOUT

Award one point for each correct answer but, to add some spice to the final round, offer a five-point bonus for getting all ten answers right but no points for the round at all if any answer is wrong. Teams can leave the answer blank.

1. What is the name of the Irish rugby club who gave their name to a kick lofted high into the air for your side to chase?

2. How many points are awarded for a try in rugby league?

3. For which annual fixture is the Giuseppe Garibaldi trophy awarded?

4. How was Gil Evans involved in the opening game of every Rugby World Cup tournament up until 2011?

5. Who is Doris and why was she so important to Jonny Wilkinson?

6. What do the pupils of Douai School in Berkshire claim to have contributed to English rugby?

7. What is the referee signalling when they raise their arm to head level with the palm of the hand open and then tap the palm of that hand with the other?

8. Which rugby player came second in the celebrity show *Strictly Come Dancing* with his partner Lilia Kopylova in 2006, beating Spice Girl Emma Bunton and goalkeeper Peter Schmeichel but losing out to cricketer Mark Ramprakash in the final?

9. Name the rugby league side that won the two-match cross-code challenge against Bath in 1996.

10. Which European side that won the World Rugby Nations Cup in 2015 plays in yellow shirts?

• • • • • • • • • • • • • • • • • • • • • • • • • • • • • • • • • • • • • • • • • •

# ANSWERS

## ROUND 1: GLOBAL RUGBY KNOWLEDGE

1. The All Blacks

2. Oscar Wilde

3. Matt Damon

4. The rugby posts – Caithness Rugby Club were awarded the posts from Murrayfield following the submission of the following poem written by the club secretary Shona Kirk:

> *Fifty years have past*
> *But at very long last*
> *Caithness will have its first rugby pavilion.*
> *But raising that quarter of a million*
> *Has left us without a pound*
> *So to get the posts from that hallowed ground*
> *Would make us the happiest club around!*

5. Japan

6. Come out as being gay

7.  George Gregan

8.  Being banned – his offences included:
    Eye gouging – 26-week ban
    Biting – 8-week ban
    Punching – 2-week ban
    Verbally abusing a referee – 11-week ban
    Elbowing – 3-week ban
    Headbutting – 4-week ban

9.  Argentina

10. France

## ROUND 2: STADIUMS

1.  Bath

2.  Exeter Chiefs

3.  Gloucester

4.  Harlequins

5.  Leeds Rhinos

6.  Leicester Tigers

7.  Newcastle Falcons

8.  Northampton Saints

9.  Sale Sharks

10. Saracens

## ROUND 3: TOP 5 STADIUM CAPACITIES

| | | |
|---|---|---|
| 1. | FNB Stadium, Johannesburg, South Africa | **94,736** |
| 2. | ANZ Stadium, Sydney, Australia | **84,000** |
| 3. | Twickenham Stadium, London, England | **82,000** |
| 4. | Stade de France, Saint-Denis, France | **81,338** |
| 5. | Millennium Stadium, Cardiff, Wales | **74,500** |

## ROUND 4: NICKNAMES

1. Billy Twelvetrees (12 x 3 = 36)

2. Will Greenwood

3. Martin Offiah

4. Brian Moore

5. Jason Robinson

6. Jason Leonard

7. Keith Wood

8. Will Carling

9. Nick Cummins

10. Craig Chalmers

## ROUND 5: WIPEOUT

1. Garryowen

2. Four

3. The Six Nations fixture between France and Italy

4. His whistle was used for the kick-off and was first blown by the Welsh referee when officiating a Test match between New Zealand and England in 1905

5. She was the imaginary woman sitting in the crowd between the posts that Jonny Wilkinson would aim the ball at when kicking for goal

6. The tradition of singing 'Swing Low, Sweet Chariot' at England Games

7. A knock-on

8. Matt Dawson

9. Wigan

10. Romania

# RESORCES

## WEBSITES

**www.worldrugby.org**
The website of World Rugby, formerly the International Rugby Board, with up-to-the-minute world rankings and the laws of the game in seven different languages.

**www.englandrugby.com**
The home of England Rugby, with everything you could possibly need to play and follow the game in the nation of its birth. Hidden within its pages, until the rebranding people catch up with it, you will find the governance arrangements, the committees and the great and the good of the Rugby Football Union.

**www.rugbyfootballhistory.com**
An exhaustive history of the game with a comprehensive timeline and delightful stories and anecdotes lovingly curated by Nigel Trueman.

# BOOKS

Benson, Richard *Rugby Wit: Quips and Quotes for the Rugby-Obsessed* (2013, Summersdale)

Douglas, Derek *The Book of World Rugby Quotations: Wit, Wisdom and Wisecracks from the Rugby Union Game* (1991, Mainstream Publishing)

Griffiths, John *Rugby's Strangest Matches: Extraordinary But True Stories from Over a Century of Rugby* (2000, Robson Books)

Johnson, Martin *Martin Johnson: The Autobiography* (2003, Headline)

Woodward, Clive *Winning! The Story of England's Rise to Rugby World Cup Glory* (2004, Hodder & Stoughton)

*World Rugby Records* (published annually by Carlton Books)

*World Rugby Yearbook* (published annually by Vision Sports Publishing, supported by World Rugby)

# MAGAZINES AND NEWSPAPERS

*Rugby Times* – Britain's longest-established dedicated rugby union weekly newspaper

*Rugby World* – The world's best-selling rugby magazine

# MUSEUMS

**The Webb Ellis Rugby Football Museum**
5–6 St Mathews Street, Rugby, Warwickshire, CV21 3BY
01788 567777
Opened in 1980 in the building where James Gilbert made the first rugby balls in 1842. Exhibits featuring original balls and pumps from the early years.

**World Rugby Museum**
Twickenham Stadium
Tells the history of the sport with interactive displays. Replica of the Rugby World Cup won by England in 2003 on permanent display. Tickets include a stadium tour.
Open every day of the week except Mondays and match days.

# ACKNOWLEDGEMENTS

........................................................

Just as success in rugby requires a great team, publishing books about rugby also takes a wide mix of skills and personalities to get them over the line. I would like to warmly thank all those, too many to mention, who have shared their stories and experiences of the game in distant corners of the internet for me to discover. I would also like to thank Claire Plimmer from Summersdale for kicking things off, Robert Drew for his captaincy and masterly control of the game throughout, the brilliant Ray Hamilton for firmly but fairly blowing the whistle on my many literary infringements, Julian Beecroft for flagging when my grammar and punctuation got kicked into touch, and Derek Donnelly for running on with the crossed t's and dotted i's. Finally, I'd like to thank all the members of my own club, Warlingham RFC, and all the clubs we have ever played against. These are the people who, for the love of rugby, turn out week after week and make this great game happen so that people like me can write about it, for people like you.

# My Life as a
# Hooker
## When a Middle-Aged Bloke
## Discovered Rugby

*'If this is what a midlife crisis does for you, I want one.'*
Luke Benedict, rugby writer for the *Daily Mail*

## Steven Gauge

MY LIFE AS A HOOKER
When a Middle-Aged Bloke Discovered Rugby
Steven Gauge

ISBN: 978 1 84953 211 2
Paperback
£7.99

**In my late thirties, it gradually dawned on me that I had become Jason's regular hooker. It was an arrangement that worked well for a couple of reasons. He didn't need me to dress up in anything particularly risqué or to do anything too vulgar, other than cuddle in the middle of a field with him and thirteen other men on a Saturday afternoon.**

Steven Gauge's response to an impending midlife crisis didn't involve piercings, tattoos or a red sports car – instead, he decided to take up rugby. What he found on the pitch was a wonderful game, far removed from the professional televised glamour of international rugby, where ordinary blokes with ordinary jobs (and some extraordinary bellies) get together once in a while and have a great time rolling around in the mud.

By the end of his first few seasons, Steven had cracked his nose and various other parts of his anatomy – but he had cracked the game too, and found a place in the club as Captain of the Fourths.

*'Steven Gauge writes with charm, wit and intelligence and real insight.'*

Samira Ahmed, journalist and broadcaster

# RUGBY
## *Wit*

**QUIPS AND
QUOTES FOR THE
RUGBY-OBSESSED**

RICHARD BENSON